Working with
Horses

D1578642

Working with
Horses

*How to get the right qualifications,
training and job opportunities*

JENNY MORGAN
2nd edition

How To Books

Published by How To Books Ltd, 3 Newtec Place,
Magdalen Road, Oxford OX4 1RE. United Kingdom.
Tel: (01865) 793806. Fax: (01865) 248780.
email: info@howtobooks.co.uk
http://www.howtobooks.co.uk

Reprinted with amendments 1999

British Library Cataloguing in Publication Data.
A catalogue record for this book is available from
the British Library.

Cover design by Shireen Nathoo Design
Cover image PhotoDisc
Cartoons by Mike Flanagan

Produced for How To Books by Deer Park Productions
Typeset by PDQ Typesetting, Stoke-on-Trent, Staffs.
Printed and bound by Cromwell Press, Trowbridge, Wiltshire

Contents

List of Illustrations

Preface

When you are wading knee deep in mud, battling against wind and sleet to catch a horse which runs off every time you get near to it, you may feel that working with horses is anything but a worthwhile career. However, when you lead up the winner of the Gold Cup at Cheltenham or better still ride in the spotlight on a Wembley winner, working with horses is the best job that anyone could ever wish for!

This book will show the reader that not only are there many different ways in which you can work with horses but there are also many different routes to attaining the necessary qualifications and experience. The case studies included in the text feature people who have made horses their life. Some have made fame and fortune by working with horses.

In reality very few people actually make a fortune working with horses but nevertheless find their lives enriched. Let me explain what I mean by this. When I get out of bed in the morning, I go to the window and although my horses cannot actually see me, they will both whicker a greeting. They know the daily routine better than I do and if I am late to fetch them in on a cold winter day, their expression is clearly one of disapproval. Conversely on a warm summer day they trail reluctantly home like recalcitrant schoolchildren! Each horse I have ever owned has had its own very distinct personality. Each one has burned this personality into my very soul so that when one dies, a part of me dies too. *This* is what working with horses is about and *this* is why people soldier on in all weathers and for very little financial reward. Horses are a way of life!

The horse industry once had a bad reputation for unscrupulous employers taking advantage of horse-mad youngsters. Some were paid low wages and expected to live in poor conditions just because they loved the horses. This however, has changed dramatically and most employers now offer a fair wage, reasonable living conditions and sometimes even training for examinations.

At the time of writing, all the details given are correct. However, the British Horse Society, quite rightly, is stringent in their inspection of approved stables and are not afraid to remove any from their lists if they fail to reach the required standard. More colleges are running equestrian courses or broadening existing courses to suit different specialities.

Horse riding in all its different forms has never known such popularity since the horse was relied upon for transport. For this reason, there will always be jobs in the equestrian industry with more opportunity to make a career with horses than ever before.

I am grateful to Paul Checkley DWCF, Peta Roberts FBHS, Nick Skelton, Lisa Rowe, Christine Venfield, PC Paul Meanwell, Ro Pudden and Cottage Farm Riding School for the information and help they have given and for allowing me to quote them in this book. I also wish to thank all the horses I have known during a period of more than 40 years: for the joy of their friendship and the enormous pleasure they have given me.

The term stable 'lad' is commonly used in the horse industry to include both girls and boys – consequently I have used it in this book, no sexism is intended.

Jenny Morgan

1

Deciding Whether to Work with Horses

Many young girls, and some boys, go through a stage of being 'pony mad', even though they may never actually have ridden a horse or had anything to do with them 'in the flesh'. They may feel that a job with horses is just what they want when they leave school. They see themselves travelling the world with showjumpers or riding the winner of a race. In reality this happens to very few people, but nevertheless many enjoy a successful career with horses without making the headlines.

Horse riding was once considered to be a sport for only the wealthy, but in fact many ordinary people keep and enjoy horses. It is probably no more expensive than numerous other hobbies. It would be wise, however, not to take on ownership of a horse without considerable forethought. A horse needs somewhere to live – a field is not sufficient – some form of shelter is also necessary. You also need access to a stable in case your horse is ill and you need to be able to afford all the necessities such as food, bedding, saddlery, shoeing and veterinary fees. So, if you want to work with horses, your best first step is definitely *not* to go out and buy one!

WHAT DOES WORKING WITH HORSES INVOLVE?

Working with horses includes:

- working in a riding stables either as a groom or as an instructor

- working in a yard with showjumpers, show horses, dressage or event horses

- working in a racing yard or with racing in some other connection

- working with hunt horses or on a stud farm.

11

The majority of people employed in the horse industry can be classed as grooms in one way or another. A **groom** is someone who looks after the horse and cares for its wellbeing. This includes such jobs as **mucking out**, **grooming**, **feeding** and possibly **exercising** the horse. The degree of responsibility varies considerably from job to job. Some grooms are completely responsible for the welfare and care of several horses, whilst others may work under strict supervision. Working with horses also includes the ancillary industries such as farriery and saddlery. The equestrian world is a multimillion business and employs people all over the world.

Getting started

Most equestrian paths have training schedules, with examinations leading to qualifications. Some have no entry requirements whilst others need O-levels or more. Later chapters will provide details on the training and qualifications necessary for the different jobs and careers available within the world of horses. We will explore what each job entails – in some cases personal accounts will describe a typical day. Each job description will highlight:

- qualifications and experience required
- personal qualities needed
- the possibilities for career advancement.

This chapter however, will help you decide whether or not working with horses is the career for you, which branch of the industry might appeal to you most and what experience will be useful before you start.

LEARNING ABOUT HORSES

It may be that you already have horses or ride them, in that case you can skip the rest of this section. For those who are attracted to horses but know nothing about them, read on.

Horses range in size from miniature horses measuring less than 10 hands (a hand is equal to four inches) through to enormous shires – with all sizes, shapes and colours in between. We have a wonderful heritage of native breeds in this country and there are many dedicated breeders who continue this tradition. Go to a big horse show and look at the different animals being exhibited – does any particular breed or type of horse appeal to you? Go to your local riding school and help out to see if you have an affinity with horses.

- Why do horses appeal to you?

The horse is a highly intelligent and sensitive animal. He also has a very good memory. For example, if someone hits a horse with a stable broom, he will have a fear of brooms. Conversely, if you have been good to a horse and had a good relationship with him, he will remember you even if you have not seen him for years.

I once had a pony which had come from a cruel home. It took me some months to restore his confidence and to break him in to ride. I sold him to someone I already knew, about ten miles away. I did not see him for about a year, until I arrived at a show and there he was with his new owners, being tacked up about 100 yards across the showground. I walked across to see him and as I got within 50 yards I called out to him. He broke free and came rushing over to me, whickering and pushing his head into me. He hadn't forgotten what I had done for him.

Assessing your temperament

If you have a short fuse and feel that you might lose your temper with a horse if he failed to cooperate then maybe working with horses is not the right career path for you. This is not to suggest, of course, that you have to be completely soft and let horses do exactly what they want – this would be a recipe for disaster. An intelligent horse accepts 'the rules of the game' and will not normally cause any major problems. Even a horse which has been damaged or neglected in some way will need discipline – but more often than not the voice is the best tool to use. A horse who respects you and knows that you respect him will be your friend and companion for life.

Horses need care for 24 hours a day, 7 days a week, 52 weeks a year. That of course does not mean that you need to be with them around the clock, but you do need to be 'on call' in case of night-time emergencies such as colic. They need feeding, mucking out (or attending to in the field) and watering *every day*, including Christmas Day, bank holidays and when you are feeling ill. If you work in a big yard, there will obviously be a rota system which allows for days off for everyone. If you are the sole 'carer' of a horse or horses, then it will be down to you. *Be prepared for this.*

Gaining confidence

Possibly the most important factor to consider when looking at a career with horses is how you cope with being around horses? If you are afraid of horses, they will know and a minority will take advantage of this. You must remember that horses are big and strong – even a small pony is stronger than a human being. If you cannot feel confident around them you had better choose another career. If you are not confident simply because of lack of experience then the best course of action is to volunteer to help at a local riding school or with a riding for the disabled group during your spare time. This will enable you to get to know how to handle horses at least. Riding lessons are also useful if you intend to go for a job where riding will be required. Some jobs will train you, but some basic experience before you start will help you to decide if you are making the right choice.

IS WORKING WITH HORSES FOR YOU?

If you have only seen the showjumping on television you may think that working with horses is a glamorous career. Unless you are a top competitor there is no glamour and even the stars have to get their hands dirty on a regular basis. Working with horses means wellington boots, shapeless old clothes, and your hair under a hat and broken fingernails. If you hanker after designer clothes, then you will either have to consider another job or wear them on your day off.

Being disciplined

An important aspect of keeping horses is that of **discipline**. You must be able to take orders from your superiors and carry any instructions out carefully. For example if a particular horse has a certain type of feed, you cannot just feed him from the first bin you come to. Different feeds affect horses in different ways and horses, just like humans, have allergies. The wrong feed might make a horse very ill.

Being neat

Neatness is also about being thorough in your work. For example, saddles and bridles (known as tack) are very expensive. If you put a saddle down on the floor instead of a proper rack, it could get damaged or trodden on by a horse and ruined. You must be **neat and tidy** by inclination if you are to succeed in the horse world.

Dealing with people

Working with horses also inevitably means **working with people** − whether they are clients coming to a riding school or owners visiting their race horse or brood mare. There is a very strong tradition amongst horsey people of the importance of good manners and of discipline. If you feel you could not cope with this then think again about a career with horses. You should feel confident about meeting clients face-to-face and be able to answer the telephone politely.

Other useful skills

Office skills also never go amiss when working with horses. You may need to book riding lessons or cope with weighing and measuring feeds or whatever.

Driving is also useful, both because equestrian establishments are often away from towns and also because driving a horse box may well be part of some jobs.

Considering your health

It is important to consider your **general health** at this stage. Asthmatics sometimes find that being around horses makes their condition worse − although some well-known personalities in the horse world are asthma sufferers. Stable work is hard and you will need to be relatively strong to lift bales of hay and bags of feed. You will also have to be prepared to work outside in all weathers. If you arrive home after a hard day's competition, the horses have to be seen to before you even have a cup of tea. Would you have the energy and stamina to cope with this?

Remembering the pleasures of the job

The plus side of working directly with horses is the amazing relationships that develop between horses and people. Horses will remember people (and other horses) who they have not seen for years. They will do anything they can to please you if you treat them properly. A horse will whicker a greeting over his stable door when he sees you even if you are in a bad mood. To see a young horse develop and learn is very exciting. That moment when a horse you have known from a foal goes out and wins his first competition is the very best feeling in the world.

The relationship between horse and human is a very special one and this is what keeps most horsey people working with them. Schooling a horse so that he does exactly what you ask him by a mere shifting of your weight and closing of your leg is an experience which cannot be described in words. Try it and see!

Self-assessment quiz

The following self-assessment quiz will help you decide whether or not working with horses is for you. If you answer the questions honestly you should be able to make a detached appraisal of your suitability. Score A, B or C (A = yes, B = maybe, C = no).

Question	*Rate yourself*
Are you interested in horses?	_____
Would you feel reasonably confident to be around horses?	_____
Are you fit and healthy?	_____
Are you disciplined and thorough?	_____
Are you neat and tidy?	_____
Are you prepared to work outside in all weathers?	_____
Are you prepared to work long and sometimes unsociable hours, including weekends?	_____
Do you mind getting dirty?	_____
Can you ride or are you prepared to learn?	_____
Do you care about horses and their welfare?	_____
Can you work as part of a team?	_____
Are you prepared to work hard?	_____
Are you of a kind and patient disposition?	_____

Your score

Mostly As – you will probably do very well working with horses.
Mostly Bs – you may be able to work with horses successfully. Maybe you should get some experience (possibly on a voluntary

basis) before you go any further.

Mostly Cs – Are you really sure you want to work with horses?

QUALIFICATIONS AND EXPERIENCE

Following chapters will detail the specific qualifications and experience you will need for your chosen career with horses. However, there are a number of other more general courses and qualifications which potential employers could well find useful and which will help your job application. These qualifications can often be obtained at evening classes and include:

- first aid and health and safety at work
- secretarial
- accounting/book-keeping
- computer studies
- heavy goods vehicle driving
- confidence building and interpersonal skills.

There are sometimes jobs advertised which combine horse care with childcare or housekeeping – normally in a small private yard. In this case appropriate qualifications would help, such as an NNEB for childcare or an appropriate cookery qualification for housekeeping.

Getting work experience

Whilst you are still at school
Whilst still at school many young people, who are intending to go into a job with horses find holiday or Saturday work with a riding school or other stables. The Association of British Riding Schools have a series of tests for weekly riders both in riding and in stable management. You would obviously take these tests using a riding school owned pony. All qualifications of this kind are worth attaining because they will add to your CV and prove at least a degree of experience. The British Horse Society offers a similar scheme through its approved riding schools.

Most schools now arrange work experience weeks for their senior pupils. This will be your opportunity to get valuable experience and to get to know people in your chosen job. Most employers will make an extra effort to take you to events and to give you information. Do make the most of it.

Voluntary work

Voluntary work is quite difficult to find in this field, because a degree of skill is needed for any job. However, your local Riding for the Disabled Group may welcome unskilled help perhaps with putting up jumps or helping to support physically disabled people when they are mounted. A riding school might let you help with leading beginners whilst they are being taught by an instructor and may well offer you free riding lessons in return. Helping at your local horse show could be great fun – course-builders always need willing helpers and you could learn a great deal.

Ancillary trades

If you are interested in one of the ancillary trades such as farriery, you may find a blacksmith who will take you around with him for a day or two so that you can see what the job is about. You would not be able to help with shoeing as it is an offence for an unqualified person to undertake such a job, but you would be able to get a better idea of what is involved in the job on a day-to-day basis. A part-time job in a saddlery shop could suit someone still at school who wants to go into saddlery later. You would learn the names and functions of different tack as you go along.

Obtaining qualifications

Making the most of school

You may feel that if you are working with horses that school qualifications are not too important – but *they are*! Mathematics will help you when, for example, calculating feed measures or fees for lessons. Your English must be reasonable so that you can write down messages and instructions and will be essential if you are to go on to further study. Even the most basic of tests includes some written work and the knowledge you can imbibe through reading books and articles by experts is invaluable.

Computer studies is always useful in these days of increasing computerisation. Although at this point in time it has not penetrated too far into the horse world, some bigger stables are keeping their records on computer and you may be required to access that information as part of your job.

Any employer, particularly those in sport-based industries, will welcome someone who has First Aid qualifications.

Getting further qualifications
Depending on how ambitious you are, you may be able to follow
your chosen path without any formal qualifications. In this case the
experience you gain on each rung of the ladder would take you on to
the next. However, if your ambitions are high, then you may need
some formal qualifications and these are many and varied in the
equestrian world. The most usual qualifications are listed below but
do look in the individual chapters for further details:

- National Vocational Qualifications Levels 1, 2 and 3
- National Certificate in the Management of the Horse
- Higher National Certificate in Horse Studies
- BTEC Diploma in Horse Studies
- Higher National Diploma in Horse Studies
- BTEC and HND in Animal Science (Equine)
- British Horse Society Instructors Examinations
- British Horse Society Horse Knowledge and Riding Stages 1 – 4
- Advanced Diploma in Equitation and Related Studies
- BA (hons), BA and BSc degree in Equine Studies and Equine Science
- National Pony Society Stud Assistants Examination
- Association of British Riding Schools Examinations.

Where to get qualifications
There are a number of places where you might gain qualifications:

- evening classes – for allied courses
- sixth form and local colleges – some of these offer NVQs alongside A-levels
- agricultural college – this is where most people learn their trade
- approved riding school – this is the place for 'hands on training' whilst working
- university – for a veterinary career or some management jobs.

You will see that even from this short list there are many different equestrian courses. There are also many different colleges and other organisations offering these courses. A very good tip for anyone going into the equestrian world at any level would be to visit the annual Equine Event at Stoneleigh in Warwickshire. It is organised by the Royal Agricultural Society and held every November on their own showground. Most of the colleges have a stand at this event and will be only too happy to give you further details of their courses.

See Appendix 1 for a list of colleges and approved riding schools.

2

Getting the Job

LOOKING FOR A JOB

To find a job in the horse industry, there are a number of places to look for an advertisement:

- on the notice-board at your local saddlery shop or riding club
- in *Horse and Hound* and similar publications
- in your local paper
- at the Job Centre
- on a local shop notice-board
- by word of mouth, through work experience or friends or family.

It is also worth applying to a particular stable or personality who you would really enjoy working for. Even if there are no current vacancies if your application is impressive enough they will keep it on file for future use.

You could also telephone or visit potential employers, but generally a letter is more acceptable.

Case study

Emma Williams wanted a job in a top horse-racing stable. She already had experience with a smaller trainer, who encouraged her to apply to a bigger yard and supported her with references. Emma telephoned the champion trainer, David Nicholson and he was so impressed that she had approached him for a job that he granted her an immediate interview. She started work in the yard the following week and remains there three seasons later. It is interesting to note that at the same time, she had spoken to three or four other trainers in search of a job – without exception they all came back to her at a later date with a job offer. This all goes to prove that enthusiasm and determination go a long way towards getting on in your chosen career.

6, Woodside Close
Brackton
Halesbury
BX12 4TD

12 October 199X

Woodford Riding Stables
Brackton
Halesbury
BX19 7TS

Dear Mr Waverly

I am writing to apply for the position of groom as advertised in the current issue of Horse and Hound.

I am 16 years old, having left school recently with GCSEs in Mathematics, English and Biology. I have owned my own pony for four years and as a member of the Pony Club have reached C Test standard. My Pony Club District Commissioner would be pleased to give me a reference.

I am hoping to pursue a career in teaching equitation and am looking to gain experience working in the industry before going on to further education.

I look forward to hearing from you.

Yours sincerely

Claire Simpson.

Fig. 1. A sample letter of application.

Replying to an advertisement

Jobs for almost every area of the horse world are advertised each week in *Horse and Hound* and similar publications. You may also find your job in a local paper or by word of mouth. Often the best jobs go to someone already known to the employer or his or her current staff, but even they started somewhere.

Sometimes busy horsey people ask for telephone calls in reply to their advertisement. If so, think about what you are going to say before you ring and make sure you are going to be undisturbed. If the advertisement requests applications in writing, then you may only have this one letter in which to make a good impression. Your letter should be very clearly handwritten or neatly typed (see Figure 1). You should use good quality writing paper – a sheet torn from a spiral notebook will bring an instant rejection. Remember, one of the constant standards that runs through equestrian establishments everywhere is that of neatness and tidiness. Many horse owners have tidier stables than their houses. A potential employer will want to know that you are sufficiently disciplined to keep up their standards.

It may be that you will be asked to fill in an application form. In this case your letter asking for the form should just be brief and should include a stamped addressed envelope. When you fill in a form, always write neatly and in block capitals. It may be useful to photocopy the form and write your answers initially onto the copy. You can then write it out neatly again on the original and you will have a copy of the details that you have given.

Preparing your curriculum vitae (CV)

You may be asked for a curriculum vitae (CV). There are companies who will prepare this professionally for you, but with a modicum of common sense and a sprinkling of forethought you can do just as well. You should include all relevant information, such as details of any work experience you have had, however brief. Your hobbies and interest are also an indication of the kind of person you are, so these should be included too.

Your CV should be typed on A4 paper. If you cannot type then a helpful friend will have to be enlisted. Failing this, there are secretarial agencies who will do the job for you for a fee. If you get a good clear initial copy, you can make good quality photocopies for future use. The pages should be enclosed in some kind of folder. These are easily obtained from office supply shops. See Figure 2 for an example of a CV.

CURRICULUM VITAE

Name: Sally Smith

Address: 10 Park Avenue
                 Medchester
                 Surrey
                 SR21 5EF

Telephone no.   Daytime: (01562) 758123
                 Evening: (01562) 753478

Date of birth: 25th April 1977

Nationality: British

Driving licence: Full, clean licence. Own car.

Education: Medchester Comprehensive School 1988–93
                 3 GCSE passes (Maths, English and Biology)

Qualifications: Pony Club C Test.
                 British Horse Society Riding and Road Safety
                 Test.

Work experience: I have been working on Saturdays and in the
                 holidays at Medchester Riding School. I have
                 had my own horse for four years and I look
                 after him myself.

Skills: I have been riding for six years and I am used
                 to handling horses.

                 I have been editing the Pony Club newsletter
                 for a year. This has involved keyboard skills
                 and dealing with contributors.

Other interests: I play the piano and have recently passed the
                 Grade 4 exam. I also enjoy swimming and
                 tennis.

References: Mrs P. Goodfellow (Pony Club DC)
                 Medchester Grange
                 Surrey SR11 7PF
                 Tel: (01562) 795812

                 Miss P. Strong
                 Medchester Riding School
                 Medchester
                 Surrey SR14 7PD
                 Tel: (01562) 795134.

Fig. 2. An example CV.

Your personal details
Make sure you include your full address and telephone number, including the dialling code. There is no need to include primary education details, but everything since the age of eleven should be included – for example, if you have been to more than one school. If your examination grades were poor, you can just quote the subject and leave out the grade. On the other hand if they were good then include them!

Your work history
If you have had a previous job then you must say so. You should include the dates of starting and finishing work and your employer's name and address. You should also briefly describe your duties and responsibilities. For example: 'Assistant groom, caring for four horses under supervision.' Not: 'I started work at 6am by mucking out...' and so on.

Do not be tempted to exaggerate your experience. You may find that you get the job and then cannot carry out the tasks expected of you. Getting the sack does not look at all good on your CV when you apply for the next job.

It may be that you are not sure if some information is relevant. For example if you had a part-time job in the corner shop when you were still at school. You may not think it is relevant to a job with horses. However, it *is* evidence that someone considered you suitable to employ and you have had the experience of turning up on time in order to hold down a job. Therefore it is all useful information to a potential employer.

About references
Before you include someone's name and address as a reference you should ask their permission. The people you ask should be able to comment on your suitability for the job for which you are applying. They may be a part-time or previous employer, someone who you have done voluntary work for or someone who knows you from an organisation or club. If you are applying for a job whilst still working and you do not want your present employer contacted then you must make this clear.

Preparing for the interview
The interview is your chance to sell yourself so make sure you create a good impression.

Good preparation is the secret of a successful interview.

- **Make sure you arrive on time**. Make an appointment that you know you will be able to keep and ensure that you have adequate directions to the venue. If you are going to a place you have never been before, plan out your route and allow sufficient time for traffic jams and unforeseen mechanical troubles. It is better to be 15 minutes early and wait just up the road until the correct time than to arrive 15 minutes late and all stressed out.

- **Dress smartly and appropriately**. If you have to ride, make sure that you are correctly dressed. This means clean jodhpurs or breeches and boots. It is not necessary to wear a hacking jacket and shirt and tie – but you may if you wish. It looks quite acceptable to wear a shirt and sweater and a casual riding jacket. This should be newly washed and not sporting the scars of your last riding lesson. Gloves aren't necessary unless you usually wear them or it is winter. If you need a whip the potential employer will be sure to supply one. Your riding hat should be a currently approved one and in good condition, with a chin strap both fitted and used. No potential employer would put you on a dangerous horse at your interview, so you can be fairly confident about your mount. Ride to the best of your ability and never attempt anything that you are not capable of. It is much better to admit politely that you haven't jumped anything that high before than to attempt something and fall off.

  If you are not riding, then you may choose to wear either a suit or smart jacket and trousers if you are male, or a skirt and jacket (or similar) if you are female. Equestrian employers would also be happy to see a female interviewee wearing smart trousers. In any case you must be clean and tidy, with no fussy jewellery, no way out hairstyles or clothes and no chewing gum in your mouth.

- **Go into your interview with confidence**. Stay calm, smile and shake hands with your potential employer, looking straight at them. Do not look at the floor, your lap or the wall behind your interviewer. Even if you are shaking in your shoes, remember the rest of your life does not depend on any *one* interview – if you just give a good account of yourself that is the best you can do. Never, ever drink alcohol to give yourself false confidence. It will smell on your breath and will mean instant failure at the first hurdle.

- **Prepare what you are going to say**. It may help to have a notebook handy during the days before the interview and jot down relevant points. For example, sometimes you may get asked what you know about the stables you have applied to – or the famous personality at the head of the stables. Go to your local library and find out what you can from the selection of equestrian books.

You will be asked about your experience. Do not waffle on for hours. If you write down what you have done in your notebook, you will be able to condense it into a short statement on the day.

You will be asked why you want the job. Jot down your reasons and ambitions.

- **Ask questions.** Write down what you might like to ask. Some of these questions will obviously relate to wages (unless they are mentioned by the interviewer), living accommodation (if you are living in) and the other terms of your employment. You will usually be shown round the stables and if you have done your homework and the yard has well-known animals, you will be able to ask intelligent questions about them.

- Take your CV, qualification certificates (if appropriate) and letters of reference to the interview.

Anticipating the sort of questions you may be asked
The following questions are examples of what you may be asked. Prepare your answers and rehearse them out loud.

- **What do you know about this yard?**
  If you are applying for a job with a well-known personality, you must do some research about their past successes. They will expect you to know.

- **What experience do you have?**
  It is important to be honest about your experience.

- **What qualities can you offer to this job?**
  Make a list – don't be modest.

- **How is your general health?**
  Be honest about this. No employer in the horse industry can afford to employ staff who are always having time off for illness.

- **Why do you want this job?**
  Do not say for the money! Never ever criticise your present employer, however unhappy you might be. You can say something like 'I am looking to move on to advance my career' or if appropriate 'I am looking for a job in another branch of the horse world' or possibly even just 'I am looking to broaden my experience.'

- **What would you do in any emergency?**
  For example: what would you do if...a horse was lame?...two horses had a fight in the field?...you thought a horse was suffering from colic?

- **Why do you want to work with horses?**
  Think about this one carefully.

Do not go on about your present job. Horsey people can tend for some reason to get talking about all the horses they have ever owned and to sprinkle the conversation with various anecdotes. Whilst being honest and forthcoming when asked questions, you do not need to feel you have to tell your whole life story during an interview!

If you are under 18 years of age, and particularly when applying for a live-in post, it would be quite in order for you to be accompanied by one of your parents. They should however remain outside the interview room during the main part of the interview.

When you leave, make sure you thank the interviewer for their time. They will normally give you some indication of the timescale for them to come back to you. If they do not, then you may assume that you have been unsuccessful if you have not heard from them within a month. Do not ever telephone the next day or at all, to ask about your chances – this is sure to put an employer off straight away.

EQUIPPING YOURSELF FOR THE JOB

For a career with horses there are a number of items of clothing and equipment which you will need to acquire.

Hat

This must be a **crash hat** to British Standard PAS 015, which offers extra protection. It must always be secured by a chin strap. You will also need a cover, either in silk or wool. Some stables expect employees to wear 'stable colours'.

Gloves

These should be proper **riding gloves** designed not to slip on the reins in wet weather. You will also need several pairs of warm gloves for stable work in cold weather. Some people find fingerless gloves very useful, for example for doing up rugs.

Boots

Whether you wear **short or long boots** is generally a matter of preference although some employers may prefer their staff to wear one or the other. Short leather boots with elasticated sides (jodhpur boots) are very comfortable and are worn with jodhpurs or with trousers for stable work. Jodhpur boots or lace-up paddock boots are worn by racing staff for 'leading up' at the races and for showing staff for 'in-hand' classes. Long boots, which are usually worn with breeches (see below) can be leather (which is quite expensive) or special rubber. They should be properly designed for riding – ordinary wellington boots are not suitable. However, you will also need a pair of wellingtons or 'muckers' (which are short rubber boots especially designed for stable work) for working in the yard in wet weather. Never, ever go near horses unless you are wearing suitable boots or shoes. Horses' feet come down very heavily on toes!

Jodhpurs or breeches

Again, which you wear is a matter of personal preference. **Breeches** are like jodhpurs but they finish above the ankle with a velcro fastening. They are designed to lay flat inside long boots. It is of course slightly difficult to wear them with short boots because you will have a gap, between boot and trouser leg. **Jodhpurs** come right down to the ankle and finish with a cuff. They can be worn with short boots, but also with the cuff unfolded, inside long boots. There are many different materials on the market – and prices range from £20 to more than £200. It is always best to go for the best that you can afford. You will be sure then that they will stand up to the job.

Potential racing staff may be required to wear Newmarket Jodhpurs. These are especially designed for the riding position that is adopted on a race horse. If you are taking a job in racing for the first time, it would be as well to enquire if you will need to purchase these.

Other trousers

You will need some trousers or old jodhpurs for wearing around the stables. Jeans are not suitable for riding and leggings are usually too thin, but if you are just working in the stables and not riding, then either would suffice. Waterproof overtrousers are invaluable when exercising in wet weather and oiled or waxed **chaps** can be used for the same reason. Recently some companies have started marketing thick padded riding trousers which can be worn over leggings or long johns for really warm winter protection. Never, ever ride in trousers without some kind of knee padding – you will regret it for days!

Coats and jackets

There are many different coats on the market, designed especially for riding. Choose one with slits at the back and a front zip which opens from the bottom as well as the top, so that it will hang properly when you are on the horse. Make sure you can move your arms adequately, including reaching up to put a saddle or rug on a big horse.

If you are going showing or hunting, you will also need a **hacking jacket**. Your employers will advise you about what they want you to wear.

Other items

Most stables now require you to have an approved body protector. Racing riders will need **goggles** for wet weather. They will also often have their own **saddle** and **under saddle pads**. For certain jobs you may be required to provide your own **whip** and/or **spurs**. When you are offered a job, you would usually be told if you needed any special clothing. Colleges usually require their students to wear jods and a shirt and tie and sweater in the college colours. You would be given details when you apply for the course.

LOOKING AT A TYPICAL STABLE YARD

Lowlands Farm in Warwickshire is a typical 'mixed' stable yard where anyone contemplating a career with horses could get a good all round grounding in equestrianism. The yard is run by Rosanne Pudden, universally known as 'Ro' who amongst other things was an official trainer to the Riding for the Disabled Olympic dressage team in Atlanta.

The yard employs four staff. Typical daily activities include DIY liveries coming to attend to and ride their own horses, disabled riders coming for lessons, dressage pupils bringing their own horses for training and many other activities. To ensure that the stables run smoothly both in front of and behind the scenes, every member of staff must play his or her part.

Ro finds that the more senior staff 'bring along' the others, training them on the job. Her staff must know how to take the rough with the smooth. Ro too has to take this attitude. Last Christmas Day, having given all the staff the day off, she found that the automatic drinkers had frozen and unaided she had to cope with seventeen water buckets three times a day! This is typical of events that occur in every stable yard and illustrates the need to be able to adapt to all eventualities.

Ro likes to run a relaxed and happy yard, because she believes it shows in her horses and this is particularly vital for her very important work as Warwickshire County Instructor for Riding for the Disabled.

The day starts with the staff feeding all the animals at 7.30am. This is followed by their own breakfast – and then the real work begins. This starts with **mucking out** and **turning out**. Nearly every horse gets turned out for as long as possible, every day. Ro, like many other long-established stable owners believes it is very important for a horse's mind that he is allowed his freedom and playtime. Lessons start at 9.00am and the staff will have the horse or pony ready for the client. Ro believes that half an hour is long enough for a client to concentrate for in a private lesson. Even the top riders only have three-quarters of an hour. Lowlands specialises in disabled riders, and riders who are nervous or who have had previous problems. For this reason two adjoining lessons are never the same, even though they will go on all day. No horse is worked on Monday or Friday – which allows them to prepare for and recover from the weekend, and no animal works for more than two hours on any day.

In between lessons there is time for office work including ordering feed and organising both the busy schedule and special events, such as a forthcoming dressage competition. The school also has to be harrowed every day. Despite having an indoor school, children are not encouraged to come for lessons after school in the winter, because it is so difficult for them to keep warm and to concentrate after a day at school.

One evening a week a visiting instructor hires the school so that the adult pupils can have lessons on their own horses. With stable duties shared between all the staff, they finish in the early evening.

Ro then does a last 'hay' round, feeding hay to all the horses later in the evening. She varies the time for security reasons and always takes her dog or dogs and a mobile phone with her.

Asked why she so enjoys teaching disabled pupils Ro says simply: 'Riding makes disabled people able.'

A job in a busy and mixed yard such as Lowlands would be an excellent grounding for any young person wishing to make horses their career. It illustrates how a good atmosphere in a yard – which is generated by the proprietor and staff – can make your working conditions very pleasant. If you go for an interview and you feel in your heart that the atmosphere in the yard is bad – if for example the staff or horses look unhappy or there is a great deal of shouting, then look elsewhere. There are good yards out there and it is worth persevering to find one.

3

Working as a Groom

This chapter explores some of the many different areas of the equestrian world where you could work as a groom.

SHOWJUMPING, EVENTING AND DRESSAGE

These three sports are combined here because a yard containing horses working in any of these disciplines would be run in a similar way. A groom working in such a yard will have good prospects and with the right employer a great many opportunities including foreign travel with horses competing abroad, first class instruction from their employer and the chance to ride the very best horses, good accommodation and often other perks such as the use of a car. Some grooms will be able to keep their own horse and compete on him as part of their 'package'. They will become known to other professional riders and if they have the right attitude and disposition will never ever be without a job.

What the job involves

- caring for horses both in the stable and at grass
- grooming and changing rugs
- feeding and watering
- possibly exercising
- cleaning tack and equipment
- lunging, long reining and schooling
- caring for injured or sick horses
- preparing horses to go to events, including clipping, bathing and plaiting

- travelling to events and looking after the horse both before and after competition.

Even if you have qualifications or experience you will still have to learn the way that your particular yard is run. Every horse owner has a slightly different way of doing things and you should be prepared to do the job exactly as your employer wants.

Although there are hundreds of yards across the country, there are only a handful of 'household names' and they do not employ as many staff as you might think. It might surprise you to know that even top showjumper Nick Skelton only employs three grooms at any one time. One travels to shows whilst the other two stay at home – for a longer show however, this might be reversed. Nick insists that a groom must be 'conscientious, hard working and tidy'. Anyone taken on to such a small team would normally have to be experienced although Nick does not dismiss the possibility of giving an opportunity to someone less experienced – but they must be very keen.

If you are a travelling groom and are at a show, you must not treat it as some kind of holiday. If you are not at the ringside with the right horse, wearing the right tack, at the right time, you will be no use to your employer at all.

Knowing what job conditions to expect

The terms and conditions for a job as a groom will vary from yard to yard. The well-known professional riders will always pay the best wages and offer good living conditions. Further down the scale, wages will be less but they should always be at least the agricultural minimum. Accommodation can vary from a leaky caravan to a purpose-built modern flat. It is very important at your interview to ascertain exactly what your accommodation will be; who, if anyone, you are sharing with and what bills you will be responsible for. If you live 'on site' you do have the disadvantage of being available at any time and with some employers you may end up doing other jobs, such as babysitting. The disadvantage of living away from the yard, however, is that you will probably need your own transport, even if you live with parents, and your wages should be higher to take that factor into consideration.

If you are required to travel with your job, and stay away overnight, you will have to get used to living in very cramped conditions – in a horse box with other people sometimes for days on end. This will inevitably mean a lack of privacy and also of peace and quiet. Showgrounds seem to be noisy all night long! You might find yourself having to live on burgers or other fast food, because even if your lorry has a kitchen there may not be time or the inclination to cook a meal. If you are shy and find it difficult to socialise then you may find this experience difficult to cope with.

Living expenses
Some clothing may be provided, especially if your employer has sponsors or tests clothing items for manufacturers. Meals are provided if you live on site and when travelling away from home. Good employers provide other items such as boots or hats to help their employees. The very best jobs may even provide you with a car.

Wages, hours and training
If you feel the wages offered are low take into consideration the tuition you will receive. A lesson from a top instructor would cost £30–£40, and often much more. Even one lesson a week could be more valuable to your career than earning more money. Apart from set lessons, you will learn far more than you realise by working around the yard on a day-to-day basis with an experienced person.

Expect your hours to be very long in any job with horses and always expect to work some weekends. Larger yards will operate a rota system so at least you will know when to expect your time off. If you are travelling to a show or event, you will be expected to work whatever hours are required and often there will be no question of overtime payments. A good employer may however, give you time off in lieu. You may also have some free time whilst at the event to look round trade stalls and watch other competitors. For most grooms, their job is their life, so the hours that they work are not really counted up or resented.

Holidays can be a problem. In a small yard it may not be easy finding someone to take over your job whilst you are away. Most competition horses have a rest season, usually in the autumn and you may be able to get away then, if your horses are **roughed off** and turned out. In a larger yard you will probably be able to have a summer holiday. The rest season can then be utilised breaking in and bringing on young horses if you are experienced, or painting and steam-cleaning the stables if you are just learning.

RIDING SCHOOLS

Grooms in riding schools have widely varying conditions of employment. You might find yourself doing everything in a small riding school from teaching lessons to fetching the shopping. Riding schools which are approved by the British Horse Society will enable you to study for teaching examinations (see Chapter 5) if this is the direction that you wish to take.

What the job involves

- caring for horses probably mostly stabled, but also at grass
- feeding and watering
- grooming and cleaning tack and equipment
- getting horses ready for customers to ride
- leading beginners on foot
- riding out to accompany a hack
- answering the telephone and taking bookings.

A good riding school cares for its horses well, because they are what make the school successful. Sadly, however, there are some bad riding schools with overworked and badly cared for horses. **The British Horse Society** and the **Association of British Riding Schools** have done much to stamp out poor standards, but if you turn up for an interview at a bad school, then walk away again. Do not feel that by taking the job you might be able to improve the conditions – it does not work like that. Supporting good riding schools is the best way to put the bad ones out of business.

You may feel that some of the horses at a riding school look a bit old or tatty. This may just be because they are old and older horses are better for beginners. If their eyes are bright and their coat good, if the yard is clean and all the horses have hay and water, then all should be well.

It is inevitable that working in a riding school, you will have to work with people. You need to be sympathetic to the nervous beginner and helpful to those you have learnt less than you have. You may have to cope with someone who falls off or with a child who has a tantrum. You may also have to answer the telephone, take lesson bookings and take the money when rides have finished. You should feel confident enough with your level of interpersonal skills to undertake these tasks.

Opportunities available

Working in a riding school could lead to other job opportunities, such as being a **trekking instructor**, which could involve travel abroad. These jobs are advertised in publications such as *Horse and Hound* for locations as far apart as America and Spain. If you do apply for a job abroad, you must take all possible precautions to ensure that your job and living conditions are satisfactory, before you leave England (see the section on working abroad, page 41). Trekking jobs in the United Kingdom are also available. You should be a competent rider, with good communication skills and preferably with a first aid qualification.

WORKING IN A STUD

A **stud groom** must be competent in the handling of horses, including youngstock and stallions. A big stud is a very busy place especially in the springtime, when most of the foals are born. **Covering** of mares takes place at this time too and the resident stallion or stallions will be receiving visiting mares. During the summer months stock will often be shown and this could involve travelling to shows and possibly, for the more experienced groom, leading a foal or even an older horse in the ring.

What the job involves

- caring for horses both in the stable and at grass
- feeding and watering
- handling stallions, mares and youngstock
- assisting with covering
- assisting with foaling and with encouraging the mare to look after her foal
- dealing with owners bringing mares and visiting their horses whilst they stay at the stud.

Assessing your suitability for this job

Stallions are more difficult to handle than the average mare or gelding, therefore this job would not suit someone who might be nervous around them. Youngstock too can be lively and nervous and need calm sensible handling. Stud grooms really need a quiet, calm disposition and endless patience. A young horse needs correct handling right from the day he is born if he is to grow into a horse which is a pleasure to own. It is down to the people who handle them in the very beginning to teach them firmly and carefully.

Stud grooms often have to sit up at night in the foaling season. Big modern studs will have close circuit television, but even so someone has to watch the screen and be alert to possible problems. They also need to be comfortable with the fact that the birth of a foal, whilst being a moving and miraculous experience is also a bloody and messy business.

HUNT GROOM

What the job involves

It is vital to examine your feelings about hunting in general before you consider a job in this industry. A number of people object to hunting because they say it is cruel to chase foxes, yet other people say the fox is a ruthless predator himself and the countryside would be overrun with them if they were not controlled in some way. **The British Field Sports Society** produces a number of leaflets to enable you to weigh up the pros and cons if you are in any doubt.

During the hunting season the job of a hunt groom is tough. If you love hunting however you will almost certainly have the opportunity to have some hunting yourself. Getting the horses fit before hunting starts is long and arduous work. For this you will be expected to be a competent rider. Hunt horses have to be turned out to the highest standards so you will need to know how to clip and plait.

During the autumn hunting starts at unearthly times in the morning – sometimes 6.00am, which means you will have had to be up at 4.00am to get the horses ready. At the end of a long day, when the horses are plastered in mud and sweat you will have to be there to clean them off, check for wounds, wait until they are dry and settle them down for the night. This can mean a very long day indeed.

After the hunting season

During the summer months, when there is no hunting there may be a chance to travel with some of the horses to parade the hounds at agricultural shows and possibly even to show a horse or two in working hunter classes.

POLO GROOM

What the job involves
Polo grooms possibly have more chance to travel than any other. Games are played all over the world and most (but not all) players are wealthy and expect to travel with their sport. You would need to be a very competent rider, as even to exercise fit polo ponies needs skill. If you are interested in playing polo, you might be able to play in some chukkas if you have proved competent and the opportunity arises.

SHOWING

What the job involves
The inmates of a showing yard can vary from in-hand Shetlands to ridden hunters and all variations in between. Many yards have both ridden and in-hand horses and professional yards will have a number of animals which are being shown on behalf of their owners.

The emphasis in a show yard is on condition and turnout of the horses, and on schooling if they are ridden competitors. There are many months of preparation before the horses get anywhere near to the ring, so a patient temperament is essential. The ability to remain calm is also useful, because the environment at a show is often hectic, pressured and noisy and you will need to keep your horses calm.

To work in a show pony yard, you need to be small enough to ride the smaller ponies at home. You will also have to be able to plait, pull manes and tails and generally turn out ponies to a very high standard.

Show days are often long – even if you arrive home at midnight you will still have to see to the horses yourself before you even have a cup of tea. However, the satisfaction of producing a show winner, especially if it is at Wembley or one of the other top shows makes everything worthwhile.

A day in the life of a showing groom
Sally works for a yard producing mountain and moorland ponies for the showring.
'We have several different breeds of native ponies in the yard, but more Welsh than anything else. Ordinary days involve the usual stable duties plus riding two or three ponies, and probably lunging two or three others. The ridden ponies have a mixture of school

work and hacking round the farm to keep them from going 'stale'. There are always a number of young ponies coming along who are being educated for the show ring at a later date.

'Show days are very long and very busy. We will have bathed the ponies the night before but native ponies luckily do not need plaiting up. Everything has to be ready in the lorry, with all the tack thoroughly cleaned and all the quarter sheets and waterproofs ready in case of bad weather. At the show, if there are lots of ponies in lots of different classes, I spend much of my time running across the showground leading ponies. However, the rosettes in the front window of the lorry on the way home make it all worthwhile.'

DEALING

A groom in a **dealing yard** will need to be a versatile rider. If you are reasonably small it will help, so that you can ride almost any size of horse or pony. You will also need to be confident enough to ride a horse which is an unknown quantity.

A spell of work in a dealing yard will give any rider valuable experience both in riding and in assessing horses for value, ability and temperament.

WORKING FOR A RESCUE ORGANISATION

Probably the most important of the main rescue organisations is the **International League for the Protection of Horses**. There is also the **Blue Cross, Ada Cole Memorial Stables, Redwings** and a number of other creditable organisations. You may think that there is also the Royal Society for the Prevention of Cruelty to Animals (RSPCA), but in fact the RSPCA sends its rescue cases to the League for aftercare. An RSPCA inspector might see a neglected horse occasionally, but generally the job involves work with animals in general rather than specifically horses.

The International League for the Protection of Horses employs a relatively small number of people and jobs for grooms are few and far between. You will need to be prepared to see some very distressing sights and to have the patience to deal with abused and neglected animals on a day-to-day basis. If this is your chosen career path, then a first step could well be to volunteer at your local centre and see if you can cope with the circumstances of the job.

A word of warning. There are a number of so-called animal

sanctuaries, some specialising in horses, who should not be supported under any circumstances. They keep the animals in worse conditions than you could possibly imagine and hang on to animals which should have long since been put down, because they are misguided in their ideas about horse welfare. If you apply for a job with a rescue centre and have any doubts about it, ask your local veterinary surgeon or your local council for their opinion.

BEING A PRIVATE GROOM

Being a private groom can be the very best and the very worst of jobs – and everything in between! If you get a good employer you will have a contract of employment which sets out your terms and conditions and this will be largely adhered to. However, it may be that you are the only employee, in which case you will be expected to help out in each and every crisis. If you get a bad employer – and this could relate to living conditions, wages, the hours you work or a variety of other problems – then you should just leave. If you put up with bad conditions for any length of time, they will expect the next person to do just the same.

WORKING ABROAD

The English groom is rather like the English nanny or butler – for some reason European and particularly American families seem to feel they are better than their native counterparts. For this reason, and particularly if you have passed examinations in Britain, it is often quite easy to get a job which enables you to work in a foreign country.

If you feel that you would eventually like to work abroad, it is worthwhile getting at least some qualifications before you think about going. For example if you work in dressage or show jumping and think you would like to work in Germany, then take the opportunity to learn German whilst you also study for your horse exams.

Once you have made up your mind, you need to acquire sufficient funds to pay for your travel (unless your potential employer offers) and to have enough in the bank to get you home if things go wrong. You must be very sure about where you are going and the credentials of your future employer. With horses travelling around the world for competitions, it may be that your future employer knows someone in Britain who will reassure you about his or her credentials. On the other hand your present employer may know someone abroad who you can go and work for whilst one of their grooms comes to England. This can often be a very useful introduction to another country. It enables you to meet other people and get a flavour of the country, and if you like it you can return there in the future for another job.

Looking for work in the European Union (EU)

If you want to work in a country in the European Union, you will have to apply for a **residence permit**, but you will no longer need a work permit as such. In some cases, an **EU Certificate of Experience** will be required to confirm your experience in a particular job for between three and five years.

The British Horse Society will be able to advise you about adding these European recognition certificates to your own. The First General System of Mutual recognition of Qualifications for example, means that member states have to recognise certain qualifications gained in England, such as BHS examinations.

Looking for work outside the EU

For jobs in America, Australia and New Zealand you will need a work permit. Many jobs are for some reason on a self-employed basis so you will need to ensure that you have adequate medical insurance, which can be quite costly. You may also be required to provide your own public liability insurance. You must enquire about these matters before you start work. It would be a complete disaster to be involved in an accident in another country and find that you should have had insurance.

Finding a job abroad

Some foreign jobs are advertised in *Horse and Hound*. As previously mentioned, you may be able to get an introduction from someone you already know. You could go for a holiday in the country of your choice and spend your time getting to know people and looking at the local press for advertisements. For American jobs, you will see that their children's holiday camps are regularly advertised in British magazines and you could write to them. If you want to work in racing abroad, then occasionally jobs are advertised in *Racing Post* and *The Sporting Life* for stable lads. Just as we in Britain like to employ Irish lads, other countries like British lads!

OTHER POSSIBLE JOBS FOR GROOMS

A good groom, particularly one with some of the recommended qualifications and the relevant experience will always be able to find work. Other possibilities for employment include:

- rescue centre
- riding for the disabled centre
- driving centre or carriage driving hire business
- tourist attraction
- civilian groom for mounted police
- heavy horse yard
- donkey sanctuary.

There are a number of specialist agencies who find work for grooms and they advertise regularly in the equestrian press.

Qualifications to consider

General stable work
There are various qualifications which could help you find the right job as a groom. To have passed Pony Club tests or Association of British Riding Schools tests is a help. Some of the colleges offer a course known as 'Young Grooms Career Start Training Scheme'. The minimum age limit is 16 and there are no educational or previous work experience requirements. This is a work-based course.

A course with slightly higher entry requirements is that of the BTEC First Diploma in Horse Studies. Although the entry requirements are not formal, students would normally have GCSE grades of at least D/E and have at least some practical experience.

The British Horse Society
The British Horse Knowledge and Riding Examinations to at least Stage 2 are considered an advantage. A number of sixth form colleges are now liaising with other colleges for pupils to take NVQ examinations alongside their A-levels. This might be another route worth considering. National Vocational Qualifications are based on practical work and full details of the examinations can be obtained from the British Horse Society.

For stud work
The National Pony Society (see Useful Addresses) runs a series of qualifications for stud grooms and assistants both with riding sections and without. If this is your chosen career path, then you should aim for these qualifications. The National Stud runs annual training courses, but these are usually oversubscribed. Possession of their diploma, which is awarded at the end of this course, is very highly prized. For further details contact The National Stud (see Useful Addresses). You might also consider taking NVQ qualifications (see Appendix 1) and particularly the modules which apply to stud work.

Summary
The job of a groom in whatever discipline is broadly similar. A good groom, particularly with qualifications will always be able to get a job. Good grooms are regarded highly by employers. It is well known that some equine personalities have the same groom for many years so that the groom almost becomes as much of a personality as the horse.

4

The Horse Racing Industry

Horse racing employs more people than any other area of the horse industry. If you are interested in racing, some of the available jobs include:

- jockey
- trainer
- stable lad
- travelling lad/horse-box driver
- work rider
- racecourse manager
- racing journalist.

JOCKEY

Useful qualities for the job

- excellent riding skills

- the will to win

- determination to take a fall and get up and carry on

- the ability to ride at the required weight

- a high level of fitness.

Most people imagine that a jockey is 4ft 6in tall and weighs about six stone. In fact whilst realistically most jockeys are small, there are National Hunt jockeys who are tall – up to six feet occasionally and who weight ten stone or more. If you think that good steeplechasers have to carry around 12 stone and saddles can weigh very little, you will see that jockeys are not necessarily midgets. Flat jockeys, however, do have to weigh somewhat less.

Becoming a jockey

To be a jockey, you have to prove yourself to be a very capable rider. Most jockeys either start as a conditional (in a National Hunt yard) or an apprentice (in a flat yard). This means that they work in the yard and get rides in races when their employer thinks they are able enough. Realistically, not all actually move on to become professionals.

A professional jockey does not work in a yard, although he or she may be retained by a certain yard, which means they have first call on that jockey's services. Freelance jockeys ride for a number of trainers. Amateur jockeys are not paid for race riding, they either do it as a hobby and work to support themselves on a day-to-day basis, or are people who do not need to earn a living as such.

Potential jockeys could not do better than to start their career at one of the racing schools. There are presently two. One is in Doncaster and the other in Newmarket (see Useful Addresses). There are no fees involved and the school will make every effort to place graduates with a suitable trainer. All aspects of stable work are taught and each school operates just like a racing yard. The horses are often retired racehorses, so that novices can get a more gradual introduction to riding.

Although the racing schools do take people with no riding experience, realistically you would be best to get as much practice as you can before you go. If not, you might spend most of your course learning to ride. You will not need any academic qualifications either, but GCSE in maths and a science would be helpful.

Becoming a successful jockey does depend to a large extent on talent. Talent is difficult to define but normally when you first start riding racehorses, people may notice if you do have this special something which brings success, and if they are in a position to do so, may well encourage you. Some people, however, no matter how good they are, never make it purely because they were not in the right place at the right time. In this way, becoming a jockey is a bit like breaking into showbusiness – but rather more muddy! As with showbusiness, once you have made it the financial rewards can be great.

Many ex-jockeys go on to become trainers.

TRAINER

Useful qualities for the job

- plenty of experience
- a deep knowledge of racing and racehorses
- a good eye for a horse
- the personal ability to finance your operation (or a backer)
- lots of patience to deal with difficult horses
- even more patience to deal with difficult owners.

Becoming a trainer

To set up as a racing trainer needs a considerable amount of money for suitable premises which are quite expensive to buy or to rent. Most trainers have had some sort of involvement with racing before they start. They may be a former jockey, have been the assistant to a large trainer or be the son or daughter of a trainer. If your aim is eventually to train, the best advice is to get every bit of experience you can before you even think about it. Owners will not send their horses to you unless they know who you are and what you are capable of.

Some potential trainers work their way up through the ranks in a stable, going from stable lad to head lad to assistant trainer. Others make their money elsewhere (perhaps in another sport) and then have enough to set themselves up. Another route might be to start as a **permit holder** (which means you can only train your own or your family's horses) and then go professional when you are established. Most trainers have to have a good relationship with their bank and an even better one with their owners. Their income is from training fees and owners want to see results – for this reason the stress factor in this job is potentially very high.

TRAINER'S SECRETARY

Becoming a trainer's secretary is a very interesting job for someone with secretarial qualifications and a love of racing. Many secretaries also ride out one or two horses, combining this with their office duties. The office is run like any other small business office, with letters to type, filing to do and wages to calculate. Most large yards now use computers so computer literacy is very useful.

STABLE LAD

Useful qualities for the job

- confidence in dealing with big, fit thoroughbred horses
- ability to ride racehorses
- willingness to execute stable duties at a very high standard and to take your trainer's orders without question
- ability to work as a team with other stable staff
- an interest in racing.

The **stable lad** is the person who does all the hard work, but who also gets some glory when he or she leads up the winner of the big race. Stable lads look after three horses each. They will muck out, groom, feed and generally care for the same three horses every day. A stable lad will usually ride up to three horses each day, but they may not be the ones that he or she looks after.

Working hours are long for stable lads. They start at either 6.00am or 6.30am, by mucking out and tacking up the first horses to be ridden. These horses will be ridden until around 8.30am when they are returned to their stables, untacked and given hay. This is then breakfast time for the staff.

The procedure is followed with the second and third 'lots' of horses. There may be fewer horses going out on the third session, so some staff will stay behind to carry out yard duties. Lunch starts about 1.00pm followed by approximately two or three hours of free time before afternoon stables begin at approximately 4.00pm. Afternoon stables involves mucking out grooming and feeding your three horses. If some of the staff have gone racing there may be more than three horses for each person to do. Whilst afternoon stables are in progress the trainer or his assistant will do a tour of inspection.

Going to the races

Going racing is not exactly a day off. You may be spared the mucking out when you go with 'your' horse to the races, but you will be busy when you get to the racecourse. You will have to take your horse to the stables and make sure he is settled. He will have to be led round both in the pre-parade ring and the parade ring, which involves a lot of walking for you. He must then be washed down and cared for after the race. Sooner or later every stable lad sees horses killed – it may even happen to one that he or she looks after. You must be prepared for this. Your fellow staff will understand how you feel and be very supportive.

What conditions you can expect

In good racing yards accommodation and meals are provided. Staff work seven days one week and five and a half the next. All staff under the age of 19 are expected to take a nine week course at one of the Racing Schools and to achieve NVQ level 1. They then return to the training yard but are still considered trainees until they achieve NVQ level 2. The racing school provides a very good grounding for all stable staff.

Going racing with the horse that they look after may involve an overnight stay or a very late night home. High standards in the yard are always expected – an owner may arrive to see their horse at any time and it and the yard should always be immaculate. Most stable lads, especially the girls take a great pride in 'their' horses and do get very attached to them. There is also usually a good social life especially in the big yards.

A day in the life of a stable lad

Sally Wilson started her racing career, straight from school, with a course at the Northern Racing School. Here she took NVQ qualifications and the school was able to find her a job with a trainer when she left. Her days start very early with staff being on the yard at 6.00am. Sally will ride two lots on a normal day, and occasionally three lots. The rides are interspersed with normal stable duties: *eg* mucking out, grooming and feeding. There is a lunch break from 1.00pm to 3.30pm and on most days, after she has eaten in the staff canteen, Sally will use the time to catch up with sleep. Afternoon stable duties include more mucking out, grooming and feeding followed by the presentation of her three horses for the trainers' daily inspection. Most trainers listen to what the stable lads have to stay about their particular horses because caring for them as they do, on a daily basis they will notice for example if one of them is slightly off colour. Work eventually finishes around 6.00pm.

Sally lives in a flat above the stables, sharing with two other girls. Her meals are provided in the staff canteen and all her bills, except for the telephone, are paid by her employer.

Sally says: 'The worst part of the job is riding out before it is light, with the temperature below freezing. Sometimes it seems that I don't get warm for days. The best part is leading up a well-known horse when he wins a good race, knowing that you have ridden him at home.'

Travelling head lad/box driver

Only the biggest yards employ someone specifically to travel or drive the box. Responsibilities include care and maintenance of the lorry/ lorries and driving to every race meeting. It is also his or her responsibility to make sure that all the racing tack is in good repair and the correct items are loaded into the lorry for the horses racing that day. The travelling lad also loads and unloads the horses and helps the other lads to get them ready. Saddling up however is usually done by the trainer or his assistant. The travelling lad accompanies the horse to the parade ring and looks after the quarter sheets when they are removed. He or she then ensures that the cooler or sweat rug is available when the horse returns after the race.

Useful qualities for the job

- enjoying driving – especially of a big lorry

- ability to load and unload horses and handle them if they are difficult travellers

- ability to ride as some yards will need their box driver to be able to ride out as well.

For someone who loves going to the races this could be a very exciting job. Normally a heavy goods vehicle (HGV) driving licence and experience of driving lorries is required. Driving horses safely takes a degree of skill and practice.

Work rider

A work rider is someone who travels from stable to stable, merely riding the horses and not doing any stable work. A good work rider is much in demand, but is *always* someone with considerable experience maybe an ex-jockey who just likes to keep his or her hand in.

Work riders are paid on a 'lot' system. Each horse they ride on a given day is called a 'lot' and the rider is paid so much per lot. At present it is less than £10.

For the ex-racing employee who has gone on to another career this can be a way of earning some extra money, whilst doing something that he or she enjoys. Since riding out starts so early in the morning, it is often possible to ride at least one lot, if not two before going on to full-time work. However, you cannot just turn up at a stables and expect to get a ride. Most work riders are known previously to the stable and are expected to appear on certain days. Others can ring up the trainers one or two days before and ask if they can come.

Racecourse staff

This is an area where there are many opportunities, although there is no hands-on contact with the horses. Racecourses are run by a manager with a small office staff. There are also groundsmen and various officials such as the clerk of the course and the chief steward. The racecourse staff are increased on race days by security staff, caterers, gatemen and many others.

Case study

Racecourse manager, Lisa Rowe
Warwick racecourse manger Lisa Rowe was, at the age of 25, the youngest racecourse manager in the country. She likens her job to that of running a small business. It was a job she always wanted and spent much of her school holidays working with Nick Lees, the Newmarket manager. She came to her present job via a Land Management degree, but thinks that Business Studies or Economics could be equally useful.

Bloodstock agent

Bloodstock agents wear many different hats in the course of their job. One day they will be buying horses for clients at a sale, and the next arranging for potential matings of mares and stallions. The job also involves travelling around to studs and breeders buying horses both for trainers and for private individuals. There are many opportunities for travel and the top agents earn very high salaries with additional commission on sales and purchases.

There is no one route to this job, although anyone contemplating this career should have a thorough knowledge of racing, of breeding and of pedigrees. Understanding how to value the horses is something that only comes with experience.

Interpersonal skills are very important as communicating with owners, trainers and breeders is a vital part of the job. No specific qualifications are necessary but a degree, especially if it is equestrian-based would certainly help.

Journalist

There are two main publications dealing with racing matters, *The*

Racing Post and *The Sporting Life*. Jobs on these specialist publications are always difficult to get. A basic journalism qualification is useful and the best way to get noticed by the editor is to submit freelance contributions. Similarly try submitting freelance contributions to your local paper if a local horse, trainer or jockey has some notable success. For any specialist job in journalism your knowledge of the subject should be very wide. This is never more important than in television journalism where you would be called upon to comment on various horses, jockeys and trainers from your own experience.

Working in a betting shop

Betting shops are interesting places to work for anyone who enjoys racing. Good mathematical skills are useful although in large betting shops the calculations are done automatically and it is just a matter of entering the information into a computer and taking the money. If there are no customers to deal with you are able to watch the racing on the large screen televisions which are part of every betting shop. The large chains such as William Hills and Ladbrooks have a management structure with the same benefits of any large company.

5

Management and Teaching

MANAGEMENT

Embarking on a management career

What attributes and skills does a good manager need?

- the ability to motivate others
- the experience to do the job you are asking others to do
- the confidence to make decisions
- the ability to get on with other people and to encourage two-way communication
- the ability to work as part of a team
- a high level of integrity.

How to become a manager

There are various business-related degrees and courses which could lead to a job in management. The **Advanced National Certificate in Equine Business Management** for example, is a one-year course with no formal entry requirements. However, anyone applying for this course needs to have had two or three years' practical experience. The course includes two options: the **equitation and teaching option** and the **performance horse development option**.

The equitation and teaching option would be useful for someone wanting to run a riding school either as a manager or a sole proprietor or who perhaps wants to go into freelance teaching. The performance horse development student might wish to work with an equine vet or other medical practitioner or may wish to continue towards a qualification in chiropractic or physiotherapy.

Students taking either option would also learn about business and yard management and gain a variety of other skills in equine care.

Possible areas for a management career

- riding centre or large riding school
- horse racing (but only a few top owners employ a racing manager)
- feed merchants
- large saddlery store
- racecourse
- other equestrian facility *eg* a therapy centre
- publishing or magazine distribution
- racecourse or event catering
- one of the administrative organisations
- a large stud.

Exploring other management routes

The classic way to a management post is to work your way up from the bottom! This could be supplemented along the way with part-time study for various qualifications.

Another possibility is to take a general business degree and keep your horse activities as a hobby. The knowledge you acquire in pursuit of your hobby will then stand you in good stead if you apply for a management position within an equestrian-based industry.

Another route towards a management post is through the Higher National Diploma in Horse Studies. This is a three-year course, with the middle year spent working in the horse industry. Students have to be at least 18 years of age and have GCSE passes in English, Maths, Biology and Chemistry. The should also have studied two subjects at A-level and passed at least one, preferably a science. They also need to have practical experience equivalent to BHS Horse Knowledge and Riding stage two.

This is a broad course with a number of optional modules designed to enable students to follow their preferred paths. Holders of this diploma would be expected to be able to work in positions of responsibility in almost any equestrian-based business.

A number of colleges also offer degree courses for students wishing to graduate before taking up an equestrian-based career. These degrees and their content vary from college to college and a certain amount of research is necessary to find the course best suited to you.

College courses
A number of the better known courses are listed below to give you some idea of what is available. However this list is not exhaustive and new courses are being added even as this is written.

1. Warwickshire College, Moreton Morrell, Warwick CV35 9BL. Tel: (01926) 651367
BA (Honours) degree and BA degree in Equine Studies. A four-year course with the third year spent working in a work placement.
Entry requirements: Students will be at least 18 years old and have GCSE passes in English, Maths and two sciences and two or three A-levels, scoring at least 14 points. They should be committed to the equine industry and have a level of experience.

2. Brackenhurst College, Southwell, Nottinghamshire NG25 0QF. Tel: (01636) 812252.
BSc (Honours) Equine Studies. This is a three-year full-time course or a four-year sandwich course.
Entry requirements: Students should be at least 18 years old and have a minimum of 12 points at A-level, including a science subject (preferably biology). Potential students who already have an appropriate BTEC or HND qualification may start their degree in the second year. This course has its emphasis on the sports horse and equips students for careers in a wide range of scientific, technical or business management positions.

3. The Royal Agricultural College, Cirencester, Gloucestershire GL7 6JS. Tel: (01285) 652531.
BSc (Honours) in International Agricultural and Equine Business Management. This is a three-year full-time or a four-year sandwich course.
Entry requirements: Students should have a minimum of 12 points at A-level and are strongly recommended to complete a full year at work both in traditional agriculture and with horses before they start. Graduates from this course have gone on to run top thoroughbred studs, racehorse training establishments and competition yards.

Other useful skills
- driving – you will inevitably need to travel
- keyboard and computer skills

- other languages, especially European
- familiarity with office technology and routine
- accounting experience.

Summary

Many people become managers by gradually taking more responsible roles in their organisation as they develop and gain experience, rather than by specifically setting out to become managers. However, if management is your aim then every bit of experience you can get in your chosen field will help you achieve your aim.

If you choose an academic route to your chosen career, then you must also get some practical experience on the way. Conversely if you choose a practical route academic qualifications will boost your progress.

TEACHING

Embarking on a teaching career

What attributes and skills make a good teacher?

- the ability to convey information to others
- the ability to ride at a much higher level than those you are teaching
- endless patience
- good interpersonal skills
- wide-ranging associated knowledge.

How to become a teacher

The standard route for anyone wishing to make teaching their career is through the British Horse Society examinations. These are taken at BHS approved riding centres throughout the country. Potential students either secure a job in one of these establishments and are given tuition for their examinations as part of their 'wages' or they may work elsewhere and study on their own. The British Horse Society does however recommend the former course of action. They publish a booklet called *Where to Train* which is available direct from the Society (see Useful Addresses).

Sometimes Pony Club members who have attained their B test and above can gain valuable experience teaching younger children at Pony Club rallies and at camp. This enables them to see at first hand if they would enjoy a teaching career.

Anyone contemplating teaching must be sure that they have the right personality for the job. Authority can be established in a quiet and firm way without any need for raised voices or threats. Someone with a quick temper would not make a good teacher. There will always be moments of frustration but losing your temper is just not acceptable. After all, your pupils are your bread and butter, so they should be treated with respect. You should also be able to be calm in a crisis and know what to do if someone has an accident. Riding is a risk sport and there will be accidents – hopefully not too often!

You must be prepared to keep your own riding skills up-to-date so that you continue to function to your highest ability. If you intend to teach competition riders it will add to your reputation if you also compete successfully.

Case study

A lifetime in teaching
Peta Roberts is a Fellow of the British Horse Society and divides her time between teaching, examining and looking after her young daughter, Georgie. She has always ridden. She says 'To have ridden and competed as much as I have would have been difficult without becoming an instructor. I would have had to have a very good job elsewhere to support me.' Her parents insisted that she took her assistant instructor certificate and this was later followed by a standard route through the BHS examinations. She also did a secretarial course so that she always had something to fall back on if she wanted a change from the mud and the cold of working with horses.

Peta is a well-known competitor both in side-saddle, for which she is one of the foremost exponents in the country, and in show-jumping.

Candidates for the British Horse Society's Fellowship examination need two letters of recommendation from other Fellows before they can apply for the exam and even then many of the candidates are not accepted on their first or even second attempt.

As an examiner, Peta says that she learns something new from every set of candidates. Her best advice to anyone contemplating a career with horses is:

1. Make sure you have another skill as a back-up.

2. Take jobs in places where you will learn and which will look

good on your CV, regardless of the wages offered.

3. Never turn down a chance to compete however bad the horse. If you make a good job of it, you may be offered something better next time.

Examinations and courses
This section outlines the examinations and courses available for becoming a teacher.

Horse Knowledge (HK) and Riding (R) and Horse Knowledge and Care Examinations
1. **Stage one**: Minimum age 16 years. This is a basic test in which candidates demonstrate some knowledge and are able, under supervision, to work with horses.

2. **Stage two**: The candidate must first pass the **BHS Riding and Road Safety test**. They should understand the general management and care of horses and be able to work under regular, but not constant, supervision. The ability to ride a quiet horse on the road, in a menage and in the countryside is also required.

3. **Stage three**: Minimum age 17 years. Candidates must look after up to four horses in various circumstances. A written test is also included. Candidates taking just the **Grooms Certificate** must still be able to ride well enough to take horses on ride and lead exercises.

The BHS Preliminary Teaching Test
Minimum age 17½ years. Candidates under 18 are required to have four GCSEs, Grade C or above, one of which must be English Language or Literature. They must also have passed HK and R Stage two (see above).

BHS Preliminary Teacher
This is awarded to candidates passing HK and R Stage three and the Preliminary Teaching Test. They then become a trainee teacher and must log up 500 hours of teaching (25 percent of which may be on stable management). The candidate then needs to gain a current Health and Safety at Work certificate before the **BHS Assistant Instructors certificate** can be awarded. Mature students with extensive experience may be exempt from the 500-hour rule.

Horse Knowledge and Riding stage four
Minimum age 20 years. Candidates must by this stage be capable of taking sole charge of a group of horses both stabled and at grass. They must be a competent rider capable of training and improving horses. Candidates passing the HK and Care section would be awarded the **Intermediate Stable Managers Certificate**.

The BHS Intermediate Teaching Examination
Minimum age 20 years. This examination is open to candidates who hold the **Assistant Instructor Certificate**. The examination covers general teaching with class rides, individual dressage and jumping lessons and also lunge lessons, general discussions, talks and short lectures.

The Intermediate Instructors Certificate
This is awarded to candidates passing the **Intermediate Teaching Examination** and the complete HK and R stage four.

The BHS Instructors Certificate
The minimum age is 22 years and candidates must already hold the Intermediate Instructors Certificate. The Instructors Certificate requires the passing of two examinations: the **BHS Stable Managers Examination** and the **BHS Equitation and Teaching Examination**.

For those who wish to go to the very top of their chosen profession, the British Horse Society also offers a **Fellowship Examination**. The minimum age is 25 years and would often be taken at a much older age than this. **Fellows of the British Horse Society** are highly respected as top level trainers, all over the world.

Figure 3 is a flowchart which illustrates the British Horse Society examination structure.

General information
A very good leaflet entitled *Working with Horses* is available from the BHS and explains the examination structure in detail.

Normally for anyone wanting to make teaching their career, a job in a good establishment would not be possible without at least some of these qualifications and some proven experience.

Some colleges are now offering specific courses for those who would like to make a career in teaching Riding for the Disabled. You should have an interest in working with disabled people, especially those with learning difficulties. You also need to be physically strong enough to cope with children and possibly adults

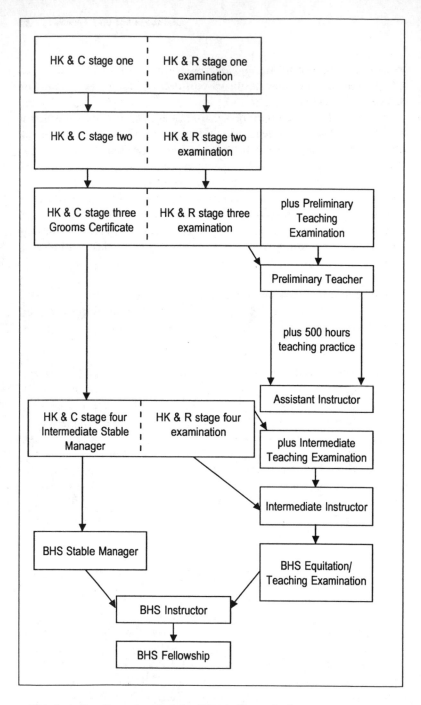

Fig. 3. A flowchart showing the British Horse Society's Examinations.

who need help mounting and dismounting. Working with disabled people can be very rewarding as Rosanne Pudden's case study in Chapter 2 suggests.

An example of a course specialising in Riding for the Disabled is one held at Duchy College, Stoke Climsland, Callington, Cornwall PL17 8PB. Telephone: (01579) 370769. The course is for the National Certificate in the Management of Horses (NCMH) and is a one-year full-time course for students over the age of 17 years. They must have worked for a minimum of one year in the horse industry and have gained BHS stage two, NVQ level 2 or Pony Club B Test. Alternatively they could hold a BTEC First Diploma in Equine Studies to merit standard or above. They must have also achieved a satisfactory standard at GCSE level and be supported by an employer's reference.

The Riding for the Disabled option follows the basic NCMH except for the riding and teaching elements, including instead training on disabilities, physiotherapy, and specialist teaching methods and tack.

Other useful skills

- **First aid**. At a certain level this is a requirement for the British Horse Society examinations.

- **Driving**. You may need to go out and visit some of your pupils, even if you teach at a school.

- **HGV Driving**. If you work for a school or want to compete it is always useful to be able to drive a horse-box (although not all horse-boxes are big enough to need this licence).

Summary

It has been said that good teachers are born and not made and most people do go into this career because they feel they have a leaning towards it. As long as you have the necessary qualifications teaching is something which you can always go back to even if your career goes off in another direction for a while. Good instructors take a real pride in encouraging young people (and older ones) to improve their skills and to make a success of their riding whether for pleasure or competition.

Insurance must never be ignored by instructors. You must either be covered by the stables for whom you are working, or you must have your own insurance. There is a well-documented recent case, whereby someone was teaching a child on one of her own ponies. The pony bolted and seriously injured the child. The woman who was instructing is being sued for massive damages by the child's family. This is a lesson for everyone who teaches, whether on their own pony or on someone else's and even if it is only for one lesson – always have adequate insurance cover.

6

Other Jobs with Horses

FARRIER

Understanding what a farrier does

Every horse and pony needs to have visits from the **farrier**. Horses who do not need to wear shoes will still need their feet trimmed and kept tidy. A horse wearing shoes needs to have them taken off and either changed for a new set or have his feet trimmed and the old ones put back on again every six weeks or so. How long shoes last depends on the amount of wear they have had and how much the horses feet have grown. Shoes vary according to the type of horse and the work he does.

Some farriers specialise in remedial shoeing *ie* making special shoes to correct problems. Shoes are either put on to the foot 'hot' or 'cold'. For **hot shoeing** the farrier brings a portable forge for heating up the shoes, and an anvil for shaping them to fit. This is the best method because fitting is more accurate. For **cold shoeing** the farrier buys ready-made shoes in different sizes and uses the one that is the best fit. He can alter them slightly with the hammer but not as accurately as with hot shoeing.

Assessing your suitability for the job

Are you:

- confident with horses
- happy to work outside in all weathers
- able to take a pride in your work – mistakes could injure a horse
- prepared to undertake a long training
- able to deal with people
- prepared to work on a self-employed basis
- able to work in a stooped position for fairly long periods of time
- physically strong?

Confidence around horses, physical strength and the ability to work outside in all weathers are particularly important for a farrier. The work can be very heavy, if you are carrying around a portable forge and anvil, and can be dangerous, if a horse takes an objection to being shod. In practice, most farriers will not shoe horses they know to be difficult – because they are self-employed they cannot afford to be off work with an injury. For this reason most horse owners will ensure that their horse is good with the farrier. Most farriers operate as sole traders, which means in effect that they run a small business. He or she takes the bookings, orders stock, keeps accounts and so on, as well as actually attending to the horses.

Understanding the legal situation

Every person who practises farriery in any form must be registered with the **Farriers Registration Council** (see Useful Addresses). This is required by law. There are various methods of admission to the register and different qualifications available. **The Worshipful Company of Farriers** administers the training and examination for the competence of farriers. It should be mentioned here that it is possible to obtain farriery training and qualifications in the army and further details of this should be obtained from your Army Careers Office.

Training

A four-year apprenticeship with a senior farrier used to be the usual route to qualification but now farriery training is becoming more college based – although still with much practical experience included.

Generally the first step would be the **BTEC First Diploma in Pre-Farriery**. This course provides an introduction to the job and if you decide to go into an apprenticeship it is then three years instead of four. There are no formal entry requirements to the pre-farriery course, but some GCSEs and some practical experience with horses is useful.

An apprenticeship is not very easy to get. The potential candidate must first get a list of **Approved Training Farriers** (ATF) from the **Farriers Registration Council**. He or she must then write off to as many as possible asking for an apprenticeship. This means the ATF supporting you as an apprentice and employing you during your training. It is very important at this stage to make a good impression and to demonstrate a real enthusiasm for the job. Many would-be farriers are discouraged by the difficulty in securing an apprenticeship but it you are really determined, you will eventually succeed.

Examinations will follow successful training and they start with the **Diploma of the Worshipful Company of Farriers** (DWCF). On passing this examination and applying correctly for registration to the Farriers Registration Council a person may legally undertake farriery work.

After two years in work, you can take the **Associate of the Worshipful Company of Farriers Examination** (AWCF). Passing this demonstrates high technical merit. For those who wish to rise to the highest levels, there is the **Fellowship of the Worshipful Company of Farriers** (FCWF). This can be taken not less than a year after AWCF and not less than five years after DWCF. You would normally take this path if you intended to lecture or train other farriers.

There will always be jobs for trained farriers. You only have to ask any horse owner how difficult it is to get a farrier. It is a craft which a good practitioner can be justifiably proud and financial rewards reflect the long period of training and the degree of skill involved.

Training for farriers continues to move forward – recently for example, there have been a number of colleges offering a BTEC National Diploma in Farriery. The Farriers Registration Council offer a series of useful and informative leaflets with all the latest information.

A typical day in the life of a farrier

Paul Checkley DWCF, registered farrier
Paul has been a qualified, self-employed farrier for more than 15 years but he arrived at his chosen profession somewhat by chance. 'During my last four years at school, I worked on a farm during weekends and holidays. This meant that I knew that when I left school, I wanted to work outside and with animals.' On leaving school he went to work at a local stables, but with the knowledge that this would not make his fortune he spent an increasing amount of time helping Nick James, a qualified farrier who had a forge at the stables. 'I was very lucky that Nick offered me an apprenticeship and I did my training with him, and at the Hereford School of Farriery. I had not planned to go to college at all, but I actually really enjoyed the academic part of my training.'

A typical day for Paul can start with taking his children to school, after which he will cover a 25-mile radius from his home, shoeing horses and trimming feet. No two days are ever the same and he enjoys travelling around, meeting different owners and dealing with all sizes and types of horses. He says: 'There is an enormous amount of satisfaction to be gained from a job well done, especially when I have been able to correct lameness and other problems with good shoeing. It can be a tough job in the winter, especially during bad weather, but the rest of the year more than makes up for it. I enjoy being my own boss and planning my time to suit my family.'

Paul's best advice for would-be farriers is to spend time finding a good farrier to take you on. Work hard to make your college application successful and hope that you have lots of luck in getting started.

SADDLERY

Every horse needs saddlery, from the very basic **saddle** and **bridle** to perhaps **driving harness** and **racing tack**. Although there has been an increase in the availability of synthetic tack in recent years, most saddlery is made of leather and over the course of time it will need attention. A good saddle is very expensive but will last longer than a lifetime if well looked after. This involves the regular checking of all stitching and stuffing to make sure the saddle continues to fit well. Fitting a saddle is a very important service for a saddler to offer horse owners. If a saddle has been dropped it has to be taken to a saddler to have its **tree** checked for damage. The tree is the framework on which the saddle is constructed. Saddles come in many different designs for different uses and a good saddler will always be able to make-to-measure for a horse which is difficult to fit.

Good **bridlework**, made of the finest leather is also very expensive. Again bridles differ according to the job the horse has to do, for example showing and other competition bridles have to be of the best quality. Repairing and altering bridlework is part of every saddler's job. Other items which will require repair are for example, stirrup leathers and headcollars. With more and more horses wearing rugs these days, their repair is also a good source of work for a saddler. In fact, there are people who are not trained saddlers but who offer a rug repair service as a full-time occupation.

Saddlery shops will also sell a wide range of horse requisites and even if you intend to work wholly as a master saddler your shop would normally be expected to carry at least a small range of goods such as **bits** and **girths**.

Assessing your suitability for the job

- Are you good with your hands?

- Do you have the patience to work on a saddle or other piece of work for long periods of time?

- Do you know enough about horses to make tack that actually does the job well?

Training
The design, and making and repair of saddlery and associated items requires wide-ranging skills. There are a number of colleges around the country offering saddlery courses, with the best known being in Walsall, Cambridge and London. Saddlery is a possible career for someone who is disabled and therefore unable to work in a 'hands on' way with horses.

Saddlers, like farriers used to be trained on an apprenticeship system, but nowadays this is largely replaced by National Vocational Qualifications. There are four stages, with the fourth being at the level of **Master Saddler**. Also available is the City and Guilds route to **Loriners Certificate Examinations**.

For those who just wish to repair saddlery, Cordwainers College (see Useful Addresses) offer a range of courses leading to the level of skill that you require.

VETERINARY SURGEON

Anyone who wants to be a veterinary surgeon particularly one who wishes to specialise should be prepared for a long training, followed by considerable experience before they become respected in their field. The various universities offer a different bias towards the animals covered in their courses (although every vet has to learn about all animals). If you want to specialise in horses then choose possibly Glasgow, Liverpool or Bristol. This is one area of work where you definitely need to persuade a vet to let you accompany him on his rounds before you embark on such a long training.

There are some aspects of veterinary practice which are very unpalatable, such as destroying animals (sometimes when they are healthy and the owner has just got fed up with them), dealing with very distressed animals after an accident and coping with vomit, excreta and other objectionable substances without rushing to the loo every few minutes. Every vet has to put up with these aspects of the job, but there are also the 'highs' when an animal they have treated makes a good recovery.

Assessing your suitability for the job

- Will you be able to cope with a minimum of five years at university?

- Can you deal with the gory side of veterinary work?

- Would you be able to cope with the humane destruction of animals, to say nothing to seeing them in pain and distress?

- Are you confident and capable of handling all animals?

Increasingly the world of veterinary medicine is becoming more specialised and there are a number of practices across the country which specialise solely in attending to horses. **The British Equine Veterinary Association** (Tel: (01249) 715723) will help you find specialist practices. For those who have been qualified for at least three calendar years there is the opportunity to take certificates in Equine Orthopaedics, Equine Stud Medicine and Equine Practice. Candidates must have spent at least two years in a practice specialising or at least dealing reasonably regularly with their chosen specialisation. For the stud medicine and orthopaedics option there is also the opportunity to go on to diploma level.

The Royal College of Veterinary Surgeons (see Useful Addresses) administers the profession. There are just six universities which run veterinary degree courses and these are Bristol, Cambridge, Edinburgh, Glasgow, Liverpool and London. A degree is legally necessary in order to practise. There are always many more applicants than places for these courses and so academic entry standards are very high. Two grade As and one grade B at A-level is an absolute minimum with different universities having slightly different requirements. The course is five or six years long. Besides working from a practice, there are opportunities for a qualified vet with an interest in horses to go into the field of research.

VETERINARY NURSING

There are opportunities for veterinary nurses in specialist equine practices. You would need to be able to cope with the sight of blood

– sometimes in very large quantities and to handle horses in distress and pain. The Royal College of Veterinary Surgeons (see Useful Addresses) is the governing body for veterinary nursing examinations and a number of colleges offer courses leading to their examinations. For a nurse in a small practice the job could well include some necessary stable work and possibly even a degree of office work.

CHIROPRACTIC AND PHYSIOTHERAPY

Assessing your suitability for the job

- Are you prepared for a long and often self-funded training?

- Do you have an affinity with horses and a deep desire to help to heal them?

- Can you cope with horses who you may treat for many months but who never recover?

Understanding chiropractic
Chiropractic is fast gaining supporters in the horse world. If a horse has to carry the weight of a rider and jump over fences at the same time, it is no wonder he gets back problems. Chiropractors are in great demand and usually have a full appointment book. The cost of each treatment is quite high, so the financial rewards can be very good.

Training
The training is long and can be financially demanding. At present would-be chiropractors have to train as a human chiropractor (for four years) and then go on to animal studies (which takes a further 18 months). The **McTimoney Chiropractic School** (see Useful Addresses) administer training but generally students will have to find their own fees as no grants are available. For this reason most students tend to be older, having perhaps worked with horses for some years before applying to the college for training. Candidates also need two A-level passes including one science subject. Also essential to this job is a *feel* for treating horses. Chiropractic is **hands-on** working with horses at its most literal meaning.

Case study

Christine Venfield, McTimoney Chiropractor
Christine chose this career because she has always had a real affinity and love for horses.

'I trained in the old school, with Mr McTimoney himself. In those days we could do our animal training from the beginning, although I am also qualified to treat people.'

A typical day could well include treating a mixture of horses, people, dogs and anything else which comes along. Christine was definitely one of the pioneers of chiropractic treatment – when she finished her training an association had not even been formed. Because she is a dedicated healer with a deep knowledge of her profession, as well as an insight into other complementary therapies, her appointment book is always full.

Physiotherapy

Physiotherapy is also a therapy which first has to be learnt on human beings. There is presently no animal-based qualification, although some colleges do offer a physiotherapy module as part of an equine studies degree course.

Training

Potential students need two A-levels one of which should be biology. They must then train at a hospital to qualify as a Chartered Physiotherapist which depending on where you study, can mean three of four years. After this you need a further two years at least of postgraduate work as a pupil of a veterinary surgeon or animal physiotherapist until two veterinary surgeons will certify you competent to work on animals. If this is your chosen career path then be prepared for it to take six or seven years at least.

EQUESTRIAN JOURNALIST OR AUTHOR

Assessing your suitability for the job

- Do you have a good command of the English language and a good vocabulary?

- Do you enjoy writing and working on a piece of writing to get it just right?

- Do you have a good knowledge of your subject?

- Do you have the interpersonal skills that will enable you to conduct successful interviews?

Training

There are a number of equestrian publications both weekly and monthly who do employ journalists. For such a job you will need to train either at college or in the newspaper industry to give you some journalistic experience. Coupled with this you will need equestrian experience. These jobs are usually advertised in the publication concerned.

As a freelance contributor to magazines, you really need to make your name in whatever sphere you are writing about. It is possible for unknown writers to have their work accepted on a freelance basis, but only if it is exceptionally good and well informed.

Authors too have to know their subject very well. To get a book published, you first have to convince a publisher that you know a great deal about the subject and that you can convey this knowledge in an easily readable form to other people.

Generally equestrian books are written by people who have had long experience in their particular area of the horse industry. Obviously, publishers will always be more willing to take a book from someone whose name is well known, because a degree of sales are already assured. However, books are written by previously unknown authors and they do get them published if they are good enough.

MOUNTED POLICE

Assessing your suitability for the job

- Would you be able to be a police officer first and a horseman or woman second?

- Would you be confident in difficult to confrontational situations?

- Can you cope with the discipline of the job?

- Do you enjoy meeting people and dealing with their problems?

Understanding what the job involves

The mounted policeman is first and foremost a police officer not a horse rider. Do not think you can join the police just to ride horses. To be accepted into a mounted division you must first have established yourself as a successful police officer. Each force has different criteria for acceptance for mounted training but to give you an example, the West Midlands force require you to have five years good service before being considered. This means five years as a police officer in another part of the service such as traffic. You are then required to complete a 16-week training course in which you would be taught to ride (if necessary) and to look after your horse. It is not essential to have any experience with horses at all before this course.

Each officer is given his or her 'own' horse to ride every day. The officer also has to do most of the caring for the horse, although civilian grooms are also employed. Work might include being on duty at football matches, parades and marches but would also include high profile patrols in residential areas, parks and open spaces.

There is no longer tenure of post in any job in the police force. This means that any police officer is first and foremost a police officer and whichever area his job happens to be in at that time is a secondary consideration. Therefore if you hanker after a spell in the mounted police it would be only part of a longer career as a police officer.

Case study

PC Paul Meanwell, mounted police officer
PC Paul Meanwell was a mounted police officer for 19 years until new regulations stipulated that every officer should change jobs every so often. So he was moved to airport police duties about a year ago.

Paul has been riding since he was nine years old. He worked weekends and evenings at a local stables in return for a chance to ride every Sunday. With no formal instruction, falling off was a regular part of his experience but nevertheless he determined to make his career with horses.

When he started, it was necessary to spend a two year period as an ordinary officer, before being considered for the mounted branch. With his training only lasting four weeks, Paul was very glad of his previous equestrian experience. His dedication shows in his winning of the Grist Cup in 1985. This is competed for annually and was introduced to raise standards of presentation and equitation. Paul was only the third person ever to win this trophy outright.

A major part of Paul's work was in the category of liaison with schools. This involved taking the horse along to a school, showing him to the pupils and answering their queries about his work. He says: 'I was very lucky to be doing a job which I thoroughly enjoyed, especially because I was able to work with horses. It was almost an extension of my hobby, but at least this time I was paid for it!'

A typical day for Paul would start at 7.00am, if he was on an early shift. The first person to arrive at the stables would check the horses to see that there had been no problems during the night. Then mucking out would begin, with the help of civilian grooms.

Grooming is a very thorough operation and any officer with a grey horse might find himself washing off stable stains. After a refreshment break, the horses would have a final check over before being tacked up ready for patrol. This would either involve 'street' patrol nearby, or 'box' patrol which meant loading the horses into a horse-box to travel to a different area.

Horses are used to patrol open areas where people could be missing or there might be other trouble, for high profile patrols in the city centre and for crowd control at such events as football matches. Paul says: 'I was always upset if my horse was injured during crowd control. It is bad enough when officers get hurt, but everyone hates anything to happen to their horse.'

After patrol, which could last three or four hours, the horse is the first to be seen to. He is untacked and rubbed down, with sweat being cleaned off and a general all-over check being given. Only after he has settled down in his stable is he fed and later on his hay is given. The horses always get the very best of care! The early shift finishes at 3.00pm.

THE ARMY

Assessing your suitability for the job

- Are you prepared to have a job which entails long-term commitment?

- Can you cope with the discipline involved?

- Have you considered the possibility of being involved in active service?

Understanding what the job involves

The army can offer a number of horse-related careers to potential army recruits. As with the police force, an army career means that you are first and foremost a soldier.

One of the best known equestrian regiments is the Royal Horse Artillery, who perform ceremonial duties. Other possibilities include farriery training and the Royal Army Veterinary Corps. Generally the areas of the army which are connected with horses are geared to only take male applicants but further details of all possibilities can be obtained from your local Army Careers Information Office. There is one in most major towns and cities.

7

Being Self-Employed

A number of jobs in the horse world naturally lead to self-employment, *eg* farriery and teaching. However, there is a good living to be earned in other ways with previous experience and the determination to succeed.

To be successful as a self-employed person you need to be:

- self-motivated

- hard working

- able to raise initial finance

- have very good interpersonal skills

- be disciplined in keeping your accounts and other records

- have experience and possibly a good reputation in your field.

RUNNING A LIVERY YARD

There are livery yards in every area of the country and running a livery yard can be a satisfying and financially rewarding way of being self-employed. You will need to start with premises, either bought especially for the job or, more often than not, rented. There should be stables for however many horses you will need to accommodate and grazing for them at the rate of one horse per acre. An all-weather riding surface, whether inside or outside is also very useful and will encourage clients. The British Horse Society produce a very good book entitled *Running a Yard* which gives you all the necessary information about legal requirements for your business.

For a livery business to be successful you need to have your yard full, or almost full all the time. This means that your customers will come to you and stay with you for a good length of time, thus avoiding you having to find new customers all the time. There are several different ways to run a livery yard.

Full livery

Full livery means that you do everything for the horse. The owners just come and ride whenever they want to. This currently costs from £70 per week.

Part livery

Part livery varies from yard to yard. You might care for the horse for a working owner during the week and they could do the work at the weekend. It could mean that you turn the horse into the field in the morning and fetch him in at night and the owner does everything else. The cost of this is dependent on the amount of work done by the stables.

DIY livery

DIY livery is when the stables provides the accommodation and possibly the food and bedding but the owner does the work. A stable and grazing can cost from £20 per week upwards.

Grass livery

Grass livery means accommodation for horses who live out in the field all the time. The stables might provide them with hay in bad weather but the rest of the work is done by the owner. This would cost from £10 per week upwards.

If you intend to run a stables which accommodates horses which would normally be expected to be at grass all the time, you should always have at least one empty stable available for any horse which may fall ill or be seriously injured.

Laying down rules

Livery stable owners should have an agreement with the horse owner, in writing and should ensure that whatever rules they intend to make (such as not riding in the field or keeping gates locked and so on) should be obeyed by all their customers.

It is also important to have a set date on which livery payments are due and to keep your clients to payment on that date. It may well be useful to ask them to set up a direct debit for the basic amount each month to your account and then only such items as shoeing would be billed as extras.

BEING A PROFESSIONAL PRODUCER

Being a professional producer is in a way a variation of the livery stable owner. This is an experienced person who has either produced his or her own horses for the show ring or worked in one of the well-known yards before setting up in self-employment. Owners bring their horse along, complete with all his equipment and leave him for the producer to ride at home and to get ready and take to the shows. The owners might only ever get on their horses at the actual show.

To start such an enterprise requires previous experience and proven success, together with capital and premises. Most customers are gained by word of mouth. They use the services of people like Jenny Weston in the case study below because of their reputation.

Case study

Jenny Weston is a show pony producer. Her yard has ten boxes and these are always full both with ponies to produce for other people and ponies being brought on for sale. She started with just her own ponies, showing them up and down the country and gaining some notable successes. To finance the operation, she purchased young ponies, mainly directly from their breeder. These were broken in and schooled over a period of months or even a couple of years in some cases before being exhibited in the ring. They would then be sold at a profit to finance the keep of the others.

People without their own stables also send their horses to be kept at her yard. Jenny and her staff school them at home, get them ready for the show and transport them there. The owner or the owner's child then rides the horse or pony in the ring. The charges for this kind of service are quite high, but do reflect the enormous amount of work involved.

OWNING A RIDING SCHOOL

To set up a riding school requires suitable premises, with an all-weather surface, either indoors or outdoors for lessons. You will need a number of horses suitable for different abilities of riders and enough tack and rugs for them all. You either need to be a qualified instructor yourself, or to employ one.

Hats should be available for riders who do not own one. Facilities for toilets and for refreshments will be necessary. Capital will also be needed to keep the horses and the premises in good order until they start paying their own way. The British Horse Society *Manual of Stable Management* Book 6, *The Stable Yard* gives valuable information about setting up your yard. As with any equestrian enterprise adequate insurance of the right type is vital.

Case study

Helen and Vernon Perry run Cottage Farm Riding School at Illshaw Heath near Solihull. Although quite a small stable it is British Horse Society approved and all the staff are training for BHS examinations. The Perrys have almost always been involved with horses and had ponies for their own children. When the children had grown up, a decision had to made as to the future of these horses who were costing money and doing nothing. They had the facilities and the horses so a riding school seemed like a good idea. They quickly realised that if you are going to do the job you would have to do it properly, hence the BHS approval. They also understand the devotion needed to run a riding school. Not only is it a 24-hour-a-day, seven-day-a-week commitment, it is also very difficult to get a fair reward for your efforts. With lessons costing just £12 for one hour you have to work very hard to make a good living.

The stables employ a number of weekend helpers who get riding lessons and entry for BHS examinations in return for their work. Some of these youngsters eventually go on to other careers but Mr Perry is always pleased to give them a good reference. They will have looked after the horses, dealt with customers both on the telephone and in person and handled money.

In order to help finances, the school takes French students for riding in the summer and runs riding holidays. The Perrys believe very strongly that everything must be done properly and the 'cheapskate approach' to keeping horses will never work.

A riding school proprietor needs to have exceptional interpersonal skills. All sorts of people come to you for advice if they've bought a pony and then got into trouble – sometimes they even try to give you the pony! Many people will say they can ride and be proved wrong in the first few seconds. In fact Vernon Perry says he can tell how much someone has ridden as soon as they pick up the reins.

Riding schools are expensive places to run and certainly not a route to getting rich quick. However, the Perrys would not be doing anything else. The pleasure they get from seeing young people come to them unable to ride and then over the years become accomplished horsemen and women more than compensates for any difficulties along the way.

RUNNING YOUR OWN BUSINESS

Every self-employed person must be disciplined and motivated. Every pound you earn depends on you going out there and doing the work. For someone contemplating their own stables, a good first move might be to work as a freelance groom. This involves travelling around to different stables doing whatever work they need doing on that day. This would build up a customer base and increase the number of contacts that you have in the horse world. However, you would need to get at least two or three years of good basic experience in an employed situation first.

To be self-employed means dealing with such matters as income tax, keeping of accounts and advertising yourself. Most local authorities offer courses in book-keeping for small businesses and this is recommended to anyone contemplating self-employment.

It is very important for small business owners to have good customer relations. If you do not get on well with people – and this includes being able to deal with complaints – then you should not consider self-employment. You will also need adequate insurance both for personal accident and public liability. The British Horse Society publishes a useful leaflet on insurance and has arrangements with a number of recommended insurance brokers.

Understanding the financial side

Finances can be the biggest hurdle to overcome. There are organisations which offer grants. Try, for example The Princes Youth Business Trust, 5 Cleveland Place, London SW1Y 6JJ and The Rural Development Commission, 11 Cowley Street, London SW1P 3NA. Your local library will have copies of the *Directory of Grant Making Trusts* in their reference section.

All of the big banks offer business start-up loan packages and will also offer advice via their small business adviser. For anyone who has been unemployed for some time, there is the opportunity to apply for a Government payment called **the enterprise allowance** which is currently around £50 per week and is designed to help people become self-employed by providing at least some money to live on whilst they get established.

Legal considerations

To start an equestrian business where there has not been one before you would need to apply to your Local Authority for **planning permission**. Even if there are existing stables, it may be that a **change**

of use application will be necessary. Anyone who keeps horses should have at the very least **third party liability insurance**. If your horse kicks the side of a car when you are out on a hack, you could find yourself with a bill. If he gets out onto the road and causes a fatal accident, you could lose everything.

If you have other people's horses on your premises you should ensure that the owners have adequate insurance and that they furnish you with a copy of their insurance certificate as evidence. Always get everything in writing, including agreements and your terms and conditions. Never think that because someone is your friend he or she will pay the bill – friends are sometimes less likely to pay you than other customers.

Self-employment can be very rewarding both financially and emotionally but you must be prepared for hard work, discipline and a total involvement in your job.

Employing other people

If your business is successful you may need to employ other people. This will involve many more responsibilities such as actually choosing the staff, drawing up their contract and terms of employment and having to understand PAYE and National Insurance. You will also need employers' liability insurance. The Department of Education and Employment can provide leaflets on all aspects of employing staff and your local Adult Education department is almost certain to run courses on book-keeping and accounting for small businesses.

Work suitable for self-employment

- veterinary surgeon
- health practitioner (such as chiropractic)
- farrier
- saddler
- livery stable owner
- show horse producer
- freelance groom
- author or journalist
- photographer
- horse transporter
- dealer.

Appendix 1
Colleges and Training Establishments

COLLEGES

This is a list of British Horse Society Approved Colleges that offer equestrian courses. There are also other colleges offering equestrian and equestrian orientated courses. Check with your local authority Careers Information Service for details of your local colleges.

Aberdeen College of Further Education, Kinellar, Aberdeen. Tel: (01224) 640366.

Berkshire College of Agriculture, Maidenhead. Tel: (01628) 824444.

Bicton College of Agriculture, Devon. Tel: (01395) 568353.

Bishop Burton College of Agriculture, North Humberside. Tel: (01964) 550481.

Brackenhurst College, Nottinghamshire. Tel: (01636) 812252.

Brinsbury College, West Sussex College of Agriculture, West Sussex. Tel: (01798) 873832.

Brooksby College, Leicestershire. Tel: (01664) 434291.

Cambridgeshire College of Agriculture, Cambridgeshire. Tel: (01223) 860701.

Cannington College, Somerset. Tel: (01278) 652226.

Coleg Glynllifon Meirion-Dwyfor, Gwynedd. Tel: (01286) 830261.

Duchy College of Agriculture and Horticulture, Cornwall. Tel: (01579) 370769.

Hartpury College, Gloucestershire. Tel: (01452) 700283.

Joint College Equestrian Centre, Lackham College, Wiltshire. Tel: (01249) 443111.

Lincolnshire College of Agriculture and Horticulture, Caythorpe, Lincolnshire. Tel: (01400) 72521.

Moulton College, Northampton. Tel: (01604) 491131.

Myerscough College, Preston, Lancashire. Tel: (01995) 640611.

Oatridge Agricultural College, West Lothian, Scotland. Tel: (01506) 854387.

Pencoed College, Mid-Glamorgan. Tel: (01656) 860202/860635.

Plumpton College, East Sussex. Tel: (01273) 890454.

Staffordshire College of Agriculture, Stafford. Tel: (01785) 712209.

Walford College of Agriculture, Shropshire. Tel: (01939) 260461.

Warwickshire College for Equine Studies, Moreton Morrell, Warwickshire. Tel: (01926) 651367.

Worcestershire College of Agriculture, Worcester. Tel: (01905) 451310.

Writtle College, Essex. Tel: (01245) 420705.

RIDING CENTRES

Hallingbury Hall Equestrian Centre, Little Hallingbury, Bishops Stortford, Hertfordshire. Tel: (01279) 730348.

Huntley School of Equitation, Huntley, Gloucestershire. Tel: (01452) 830440.

Talland School of Equitation, Cirencester, Gloucestershire. Tel: (01285) 652318.

Tong Riding Centre Ltd, Church Farm, Tong, Shifnal, Shropshire. Tel: (01902) 372352.

Wellington Riding Ltd, Heckfield, Basingstoke, Hampshire. Tel: (01734) 326308.

Yorkshire Riding Centre, Markington, Harrogate, Yorkshire. Tel: (01765) 677207.

Appendix 2
National Vocational Qualifications

The complete syllabus with full details of all sections is available from the British Horse Society Training Office.

NVQ LEVEL 1 – HORSE CARE

Unit number	Unit title	Elements
3.22	Assisting with routine care	1. Maintain accommodation
		2. Provide food and water
		3. Maintain saddlery and clothing
3.32	Servicing facilities	1. Receive and store food and bedding
		2. Maintain yards and surrounding areas
3.41	Handling horses from the ground	1. Release horses into enclosures
		2. Catch horses
3.43	Preparing horses for use under supervision	1. Carry out pre- and post-exercise routine
		2. Clean and groom horses

| 3.64 | Liaison with callers and colleagues | 1. Receive and assist callers |
| | | 2. Maintain working relations with other members of staff |

In order to gain this qualification the candidate must achieve all the mandatory units.

NVQ/SVQ LEVEL 2 – HORSE CARE

Mandatory units

Unit number	Unit title	Elements
3.23	Providing routine care	1. Select and provide food and water
		2. Apply and fit horse clothing
3.44	Preparing horses for use	1. Improve the appearance of a horse
		2. Clean and groom horses
		3. Carry our pre- and post-exercise preparations
3.21	Determining health and condition	1. Present horse for health care
		2. Assess horse for health
		3. Recognise simple lameness
		4. Recognise health problems
3.42	Working the horse from the ground	1. Present horse for routine inspection
		2. Exercise a quiet horse from the ground

IACH7210	Contribute to providing grass and water for grazing animals	1. Provide grass and water for grazing livestock
		2. Maintain environment for grazing livestock
3.46	Assisting with the transport- ation of horses	1. Prepare vehicle for transport- ing horses
		2. Load and unload horses for transportation by road
IACH1010	Develop and maintain personal effect- iveness	1. Establish and maintain good relations with other people at work
		2. Managing and developing self
		3. Operate safely in the work- place

Optional units

3.51	Riding horses	1. Ride horses on the road
		2. Maintain control of a horse when jumping
		3. Ride a schooled horse

The following unit is offered through the Heavy Horse Training Committee (administered by the BHS):

| 3.57 | Assisting with working horses | 1. Hitch up and adjust harness for work |
| | | 2. Work horse in harness |

Breeding units

| 3.11 | Assisting with the instigation of reproduction | 1. Assist in teasing and covering |
| | | 2. Keep simple stud records |

3.13	Assisting with parturition care	1. Give basic assistance towards foaling
3.15	Assisting with rearing of youngstock	1. Assist in handling mare and foal

In order to gain the complete qualification the candidate must achieve all the mandatory units and one group of optional units.

NVQ/SVQ LEVEL 3 – HORSE CARE AND MANAGEMENT
Mandatory units

Unit number	Unit title	Element
3.25	Resolving health and condition problems	1. Establish cause of health problems
		2. Treat health problems
3.24	Monitoring routine care	1. Maintain stocks of feed supplies
		2. Specify diet
		3. Provide routine health care
3.47	Transporting horses	1. Prepare for transport
		2. Care of horse during transit
SM4	Contribute to the training and development of teams, individuals and self to enhance performance	1. Contribute to planning the and training and development of teams and individuals
		2. Contribute to training and development activities for teams and individuals

3. Contribute to the assessment of teams and individuals against training and development objectives

4. Develop oneself within the job

SM5   Contribute to the planning, organisation and evaluation of work

1. Contribute to planning work activities and methods to achieve objectives

2. Organise work and assist in the evaluation of work

3. Provide feedback on work performance to teams and individuals

SM6   Create, maintain and enhance productive working relationships

1. Create and enhance productive working relationships with colleagues and those for whom one has a supervisory responsibility

2. Enhance productive working relationships with one's immediate manager

3. Identify and minimise interpersonal conflict

4. Contribute to the implementation of disciplinary and grievance procedures

Optional units

3.45   Preparing horses for work

1. Improve appearance of horse

2. Tack up horse for specialist work

3. Clip horses

3.52	Riding horses to maintain training	1. Provide exercise programme for horse
		2. Improve performance of horse
		3. Ride a schooled horse
		4. Jump a schooled horse

Group B – offered by the Heavy Horse Training Committee (administered by the BHS)

3.58A	Working horses	1. Work a pair of horses
		2. Prepare and use horse in woodland maintenance
		3. Maintain horsedrawn vehicles and implements
3.59	Driving horses on the road	1. Prepare horse and vehicle for road use
		2. Carry out road driving manoeuvres
		3. Attend to horse and vehicle after driving

Group C

3.12	Instigating reproduction	1. Establish pregnancy in mare
		2. Maintain stud documentation
		3. Routine handling of stallions
3.14	Providing parturition care	1. Attend to mare and foal during foaling
3.16	Rearing youngstock	1. Maintain care of mare and foal
		2. Train youngstock

Additional units

2ACH7210	Provide grazing and water	1. Provide grass and water for grazing youngstock
3.57B	Provide trekking opportunities	1. Prepare for a trek
		2. Escort trek
		3. Care for horses on return from trek
3.33	Improving facilities	1. Maintain fences

Assessors for the following unit must be trained to RDA requirements.

3.58B	Assisting disabled riders	1. Selection and preparation of horse and rider
		2. Assisting through mounting
		3. Assisting the riding process
		4. Dismounting and debriefing

In order to gain the complete qualification the candidate must achieve all the mandatory units and one group of optional units. Additional units may be required for employment purposes, but do not form part of the qualification.

Appendix 3
Working Pupil Contracts

The working pupil system is one which has been open to much abuse over the years. Indeed there is Trade Union opposition to the system. However, it has been operated for many years by riding schools. Basically, it means that pupils work in return for their tuition for examinations, notably the British Horse Society exams.

There are no mandatory guidelines for implementation of these contracts but anyone contemplating such an arrangement should have it in writing. Specimen contracts are available from The British Horse Society. All contracts should be signed by the employer, the pupil (and the parents if the pupil is under 18 years of age). The British Horse Society offers the following as guidelines for inclusion in the contract:

- financial arrangements

- hours of work

- a broad description of the duties which the working pupil is expected to perform

- details of a probationary period if there is to be one

- details of holidays and time off

- the exact amount of mounted and dismounted training which the pupil can expect to receive, including teaching experience (if relevant)

- food and accommodation

- keeping of a pupil's horse

- expectations regarding competitions or hunting *etc*

- disciplinary rules, including dress *etc*.

Glossary

At grass. A horse living solely in a field.

Bedding. Is what the horse has on his stable floor to collect the droppings and soak up urine and for him to lie down on. Bedding can be straw, wood shavings, shredded paper or hemp.

Bridle. The leather straps by which you control the horse when riding him.

Chaps. Leather overtrousers.

Covering. Mating of mare with stallion.

Dressage. Training of horses in obedience and deportment.

Equitation. Horsemanship.

Equestrian. Relative to horses or a person who rides horses.

Farriery. The art of shoeing horses and generally attending to their feet.

Grazing. This is a term applied to horses eating grass and to the field where they do it. For example, 'good grazing' would be a field particularly suitable for horses with good grass available for them.

Groom. A person who cares for horses or the action of cleaning a horse with a brush.

Headcollar. A harness made from nylon or leather, fitting onto the head of the horse, which is used to lead him when he is not wearing a bridle.

Horse-box. A lorry which is used for the purpose of transporting horses by road. Not to be confused with 'box' meaning stable.

Horse and Hound. A weekly publication, widely available with a comprehensive classified advertisement section.

Livery stable. A place where horses are kept and their owners pay the stable owner to keep them there.

Loriner. This is a word, now somewhat old fashioned, to describe someone who makes harness and saddlery.

Lunge lessons. This is a lesson given by an instructor who controls the horse by way of a long rope (lunge line) so that the rider can concentrate on their position *etc* without having to steer the horse.

Menage. An enclosed area for riding. It can also have a roof and be referred to as a covered school or indoor arena.

Mucking out. The task of cleaning out stables.

Pony club. A national organisation that encourage young riders.

Producer. Someone who looks after and schools a horse and gets him ready for the show ring for his owner, who pays for this service.

Riding school. A place where riding is taught for commercial gain. Can also be used to denote a covered area for riding.

Saddler. A person who makes or mends saddlery.

Saddlery. The saddle and bridle and other items such as a martingale or breast girth worn by a horse when he is ridden.

Saddling up. Putting on the saddle, weight cloths, breast girth and so on of a horse just before racing.

Stabled. A horse living for most of its time in a stable. He may spend part of the time in a field but would still be classed as stabled.

Stable lad. This is a male or female groom working in racing.

Stallion. An adult male horse.

Stud. A place where horses are bred.

Tack. This term covers the saddle, bridle and any other items which the horse wears when he is ridden, such as boots, martingale and so on (see saddlery).

Tacking up. Putting on the saddle, bridle, and any other items such as boots before the horse is ridden.

Trainer. Generally used to describe any person who trains others. Also used specifically to describe a person who supervises the training and management of racehorses.

Trekking. Riding across country usually on very quiet and experienced horses. Trekking is often done in holiday areas and by inexperienced riders.

Whicker. This is the low friendly noise that horse makes when greeting humans or other horses that he knows.

Working pupil. One who works partly or wholly in exchange for instruction.

Yard. Buildings and land used for the purpose of keeping horses either for private or commercial use.

Further Reading

Manual of Stable Management British Horse Society (Kenilworth Press).
   Book 1 – *The Horse*
   Book 2 – *Care of the Horse*
   Book 3 – *The Horse at Grass*
   Book 4 – *Saddlery*
   Book 5 – *Specialist Care of the Competition Horse*
   Book 6 – *The Stable Yard*
   Book 7 – *Watering and Feeding*
A Career in the Horse Industry, Laura Collins (Kenilworth Press).
Care of the Competition Horse, Sarah Pilliner (Batsford).
Getting Horses Fit, Sarah Pilliner (Blackwell).
Horse and Stable Management, Jeremy Houghton Brown and Vincent Powell Smith (Blackwell).
Horse Business Management, J. Houghton Brown and V. Powell Smith (Blackwell).
Horse Nutrition and Feeding, Sarah Pilliner (Blackwell).
Horse Rider's Handbook, Monty Mortimer (David & Charles).
Illustrated Guide to Horse Tack, Susan McBane (David & Charles).
Manual of Equitation, British Horse Society (Kenilworth Press).
Threshold Picture Guide Series
   Fitting Tack, No. 4
   Beds and Bedding, No. 9
   Feeds and Feeding, No. 10
   First Aid, No. 12
   Safety, No. 14
   Mouths and Bits, No. 15
   Feet and Shoes, No. 16
   Grooming, No. 21

Useful Addresses

The Association of British Riding Schools, 38–40 Queen Street, Penzance, Cornwall TR18 2SL. Tel: (01736) 369440.

British Horse Racing Training Board, Suite 16, Unit 8, Kings Court, Willie Snaith Road, Newmarket, Suffolk CB8 7SG. Tel: (01638) 560782

British Horse Society, Stoneleigh Deer Park, Kenilworth, Warks. CV8 2XZ Tel: (01926) 707700. Fax: (01926) 707800. Email: *enquiry@bhs.org.uk* Web site: *www.bhs.org.uk*

British Racing School, Snailwell Road, Newmarket, Suffolk CB8 7NU. Tel: (01638) 665103.

British Show Jumping Association, NAC, Stoneleigh Park, Kenilworth, Warks. CV8 2LR. Tel: (01203) 698800.

Farriers Registration Council, Sefton House, Adams Court, Newark Road, Peterborough, Cambridgeshire PE1 5PP. Tel: (01733) 319911.

The Jockey Club, 43 Portman Square, London SW10 0EN. Tel: (0171) 486 4921.

Joint National Horse Education and Training Council, The Stables, Rossington Hall, Great North Road, Doncaster DN11 0HN. Tel: (01302) 864242.

The McTimoney Chiropractic School, 14 Park End Street, Oxford OX1 1HH. Tel: (01865) 246786.

The National Pony Society, Willingdon House, 102 High Street, Alton, Hampshire GU34 1EN. Tel: (01420) 88333.

The National Stud, Newmarket, Suffolk CB8 OXE. Tel: (01638) 663464.

The Pony Club, address as BHS above. Tel: (01203) 698300.

The Royal College of Veterinary Surgeons, 32 Belgrave Square, London SW1X 8QP. Tel: (0171) 235 4971.

The Royal Veterinary College, University of London, Royal College Street, Campden Town, London NW1 0TU. Tel: (0171) 387 2898.

The Society of Master Saddlers, Kettles Farm, Mickfield, Stowmarket, Suffolk IP14 6BY. Tel: (01449) 711642.

Warwickshire College for Equine Studies, Moreton Hall, Moreton Morrell, Warwick CV35 9BL. Tel: (01926) 318333.

The most important publication for anyone working in the horse industry is:

The British Equestrian Directory available direct from Wothersome Grange, Bramham, Nr Wetherby, West Yorkshire LS23 6LY. Tel: (01132) 892267. It is available in bookshops including the British Horse Society bookshop at the Stoneleigh Deer Park, Kenilworth, Warwickshire.

Index